ENA VISMAY

Contents

Prologue: Stones That Remember

India does not merely remember history—she lives within it, and nowhere is this more vividly true than in her forts. You'll see them from train windows and winding highways—stone silhouettes rising from hilltops, crouched by rivers, or gazing into the sea. Sometimes grand and restored, sometimes silent and crumbling, these forts are not just relics of bygone eras, they are a part of our identities, our roots. They are battlegrounds, temples, homes, prisons, observatories, and stage sets where the country's greatest dramas have been played out. They are also, in a quiet way, one of India's most unifying legacies—scattered across every state, built by kings of every faith, shaped by climates as varied as the desert winds of Jaisalmer and the monsoon-fed slopes of Kerala.

Yet despite their ubiquity, India's forts are often seen only in parts—an Instagram moment here, a dusty plaque here, a paragraph in a webpage or a travelog there, or a guide's (mostly self-proclaimed) brief narrative reduced to names and dates. This book is an attempt to offer something more: not a comprehensive catalogue, not a dry historical inventory, but a curated journey through sixty of India's most remarkable forts—each one chosen not only for its architectural or military significance but for the myriads of stories it holds, the emotions it stirs, and the truths it still dares to whisper.

Every fort is born of anxiety. Whether constructed in anticipation of siege, to guard a coastline, to mark a capital, or to imprison a rival, these were not built for leisure but to outlast. But what makes Indian forts unique is how often they exceeded their functions. At Amber, Rajput pride mingles with Rajput poetics. At the Red Fort, imperial architecture becomes a stage for a nation's birth. At Daulatabad, the landscape itself is weaponized. At Srirangapatna, resistance sings in every bullet-pocked wall. These are not simply fortified enclosures; they are canvases for art, archives of evolving military technology, and symbols—of supremacy, of struggle, of sovereignty. More than that, they are narratives in stone. A wall widened during one reign, a gateway renamed by the next. A Mughal dome inserted beside a Hindu mandapa. If you read closely enough, each one reveals how power was imagined, challenged, and performed.

This book moves not according to chronological precision, but according to narrative rhythm. We move like a traveler might—letting one story lead into another, using connecting threads of politics, culture, architecture, and even emotion to guide the reader from chapter to chapter.

From the sandstone pride of Mehrangarh to the windswept defiance of Rohtasgarh, from the sea-facing bastions of Sindhudurg to the stepped courtyards of Orchha, we travel across centuries and topographies. Some are famed UNESCO sites, others are half-forgotten and barely marked on maps. What unites them is not just stones, but stories. Within these stories lie deep contradictions. The same fort might be remembered as a seat of justice and a place of betrayal. It might have housed a resistance movement in one era and a colonial prison in the next. The ghosts do not agree. That's what makes them worth visiting.

This book is not an architectural survey, though the architecture will awe you. It is not a military treatise, though the strategies will fascinate you. It is not a tourist guide, though it might inspire your next itinerary. What it is, is a portrait gallery. Sixty distinct profiles, each told with care, curiosity, and historical grounding. These portraits move between facts and feelings, stones and stories, past and present. Each entry is anchored by a pithy title, a declared period of relevance, and a narrative that captures the fort's essence without drowning the reader in dates. We hope you find the personality of each place—some austere, some romantic, some paranoid, some playful.

The book deliberately includes forts from every cultural corner—Rajput, Mughal, Maratha, Sikh, Portuguese, British, Mysorean, Tamil, and more. This is because India's story was never singular. Her political map has always been a mosaic. And so her forts, too, reflect a wide spectrum of intent, design, and legacy. Some were built by those who ruled. Others were claimed by those who resisted. Some were lost overnight in betrayal; others held out for years. Some changed hands so often they became palimpsests—layer upon layer of rulers, religions, regimes. But all of them, in their own way, witnessed the making of India.

Today, many of these forts face a different kind of siege—not from armies, but from apathy. Encroachment, neglect, and thoughtless development threaten structures that once shaped kingdoms. And yet, hope remains. Heritage movements, conservation architects, state agencies, and community efforts are beginning to restore not just the stones, but the stories.

If this book succeeds in anything, let it be this: that you begin to look at forts not as mute ruins, but as vital interlocutors between history and modernity. That you see them not only with your eyes, but with your imagination. That you seek them out—not just the famous ones, but the lonely ones, the half-forgotten ones, the ones whose names don't appear in textbooks.

Because every fort you visit is a conversation. With a time, a ruler, a community, a vision of the world. And India, as this book will show you, is still listening—one amazing fort at a time.

Red Fort, Delhi

Where Empires Marched and Nations Began

(Mughal Period to Indian Independence: 17th–20th centuries)

On the ramparts of the Red Fort, emperors once watched the sun rise over a subcontinent they believed invincible. Centuries later, a man in homespun khadi stood at the same spot and announced that India was free. Few structures bear the weight of so much history, ceremony, and symbolism.

Commissioned by Emperor Shah Jahan in 1638, the Red Fort—Lal Qila—was the centerpiece of his new capital, Shahjahanabad, named after the red sandstone that forms its imposing walls. Within those walls unfolded a world of intricate marble inlay, mirrored ceilings, gardens laid out in geometric precision, and the fabled Diwan-i-Khas—where it was said that if there was a paradise on earth, 'it was here, it was here, it was here.'

Less than 150 years after it was built, the fort was plundered by Nadir Shah of Persia, who carried away the Peacock Throne. In 1857, during the First War of Independence, it became the site of the last desperate stand of the Mughal dynasty. Bahadur Shah Zafar, poet-king and reluctant rebel, was tried here before being exiled to Rangoon. British troops occupied the fort thereafter, turning its halls into barracks. Even so, the Red Fort remained—watching, absorbing. It stood through famines, curfews, and two world wars. In 1947, when Jawaharlal Nehru unfurled the Indian tricolor from its ramparts, the fort became more than a monument. Every year since, on Independence Day, the Prime Minister ascends its walls and addresses the nation.

Architecturally, the Red Fort layout balances symmetry with surprise—bazaars that open into gardens, pavilions that lead into shadowy courtyards. The Mughal aesthetic, steeped in Persian influence but adapted to Indian materiality, finds here one of its most magnificent expressions.

Today, it lives as a UNESCO World Heritage Site, a museum, and a site of both protest and pageantry. It is where tourists line up for selfies, soldiers stand guard, and generations of Indians hear speeches that begin with a salutation to the past.

The Red Fort is not just where Delhi once ruled India. It is where India continues to speak to itself—of its past empires, its hopes, and its future.

Agra Fort, Uttar Pradesh

The Throne Before the Throne

(Mughal Zenith: 16th–17th centuries)

Before Delhi, there was Agra. And before Shah Jahan dreamed of marble and minarets, his grandfather Akbar built his empire in red sandstone—firm, grounded, and vast. Agra Fort was not only the Mughals' first imperial seat in India, but it was where their dynasty defined itself.

Built on the banks of the Yamuna, the fort, as we know it, began in 1565 under Akbar's rule. A military strategist as much as a statesman, he chose the site for its defensive advantages and proximity to trade routes—but what he built went far beyond defense. The original fort, known in earlier centuries as Badalgarh, was razed and replaced by a fortress-palace that fused strength with splendor.

Under Akbar, Agra Fort housed courtyards, mosques, audience halls, and the private chambers of a ruler who believed in debate more than decree. Under Jahangir, it became a place of pleasure and poetry. Under Shah Jahan, it transformed again—stone gave way to marble, walls grew lighter, and elegance replaced austerity. Ironically, it was also here that Shah Jahan would spend his final years—imprisoned by his son Aurangzeb, gazing across the river at the white tomb he built for his beloved Mumtaz.

The fort was a seat of governance and diplomacy. It saw embassies from Europe, heard court musicians and poets, and bore witness to the inner workings of a dynasty at its peak. The Diwan-i-Aam and Diwan-i-Khas, much like those later built in Delhi, were stages where the Mughal court displayed its blend of theatricality and bureaucracy. Unlike the Red Fort, Agra's walls feel heavier, older, and more weathered by time. Its double ramparts and four imposing gates—especially the Amar Singh Gate, still in use—speak of a fortress first, a palace second. And yet, within its 94-acre perimeter lie stories of love, betrayal, ambition, and loss. Here, princes plotted, emperors judged, and history took its time to shape and reshape itself.

Today, Agra Fort is a UNESCO World Heritage Site, often overshadowed by the Taj Mahal just a few kilometers away. But those who linger within its walls feel the pulse of an empire in full possession of its destiny.

Fatehpur Sikri, Uttar Pradesh

The City That Echoes an Emperor's Dream

(Mughal Empire under Akbar, 16th century)

If Delhi was the seat of empire and Agra its vault, Fatehpur Sikri was to be its soul. Commissioned in 1571 by Emperor Akbar, the city was built to honor the Sufi saint Sheikh Salim Chishti, who had foretold the birth of Akbar's long-awaited heir. In gratitude, Akbar decided not just to erect a shrine, but to build an entire capital around it.

What emerged from the dry plateau near Agra was one of the most exquisite urban expressions of the Mughal imagination. Part citadel, part palace, part spiritual retreat, Fatehpur Sikri was a grand experiment in governance, culture, and faith. For fourteen heady years, it was the center of the Mughal world.

The city was laid out with meticulous symmetry and infused with eclecticism. Persian arches met Hindu *chhatris*. Jain motifs stood beside Islamic inscriptions. Akbar, whose court was famously pluralistic, invited scholars of all faiths to debate in the Ibadat Khana, the Hall of Worship. His Din-i-Ilahi, a syncretic spiritual philosophy, was born here—an attempt to unify India's religious spectrum under one umbrella.

At the heart of Fatehpur Sikri lies the Buland Darwaza, the 54-meter-high gateway that dwarfs all who enter. Built to commemorate Akbar's conquest of Gujarat, it remains one of the grandest doorways in the world. Within its embrace unfolds a city of wonders: the Diwan-i-Khas, with its famed central pillar from which Akbar presided like a philosopher-king; the Diwan-i-Aam, for public audiences; the airy Panch Mahal, where queens once lingered behind lattice; and the white marble dargah of Sheikh Salim Chishti, still reverently visited today.

By 1585, Akbar abandoned Fatehpur Sikri, allegedly due to water scarcity, strategic concerns, or simply imperial drift. The capital shifted to Lahore. The red sandstone palaces, untouched by later reconstructions, remain remarkably intact. Today, the city is a UNESCO World Heritage Site, and though not a fort in the traditional sense, in its brief life, Fatehpur Sikri asked: can an emperor govern not just land, but belief?

Chittorgarh Fort, Rajasthan

The Flame That Refused to Die

(Rajput Resistance: 7th–16th centuries)

Chittorgarh is not just a fort. It is a memory—scarred, sung, and seared into the Indian imagination. Spread across a 700-acre plateau in southern Rajasthan, it rises like a great, slumbering beast—wounded yet watchful. Here, tales are not told in stone alone, but in song, in silence, and the faint scent of ash on the wind.

Founded in the 7th century by the Maurya dynasty and later seized by the Sisodia Rajputs of Mewar, Chittorgarh became not just a capital, but a crucible of honor. Of resistance. Of refusal. For nearly a millennium, it stood as the heart of Rajput valor—a defiant redoubt against the tide of imperial ambition that swept through northern India.

Three times it fell. Each time, not with surrender, but with *jauhar*. In 1303, Alauddin Khilji laid siege in pursuit, legend says, of the peerless Rani Padmini. When defeat was inevitable, the women committed self-immolation; the men rode out to die. In 1535, Bahadur Shah of Gujarat besieged it again—*jauhar* followed. In 1567, Akbar came. The siege lasted four months. Again, the flames rose.

Chittorgarh today is a sprawl of ruins, towers, temples, and echoes. The Vijay Stambh—the Tower of Victory—built by Rana Kumbha in the 15th century to celebrate his triumph over Malwa and Gujarat, stands like a defiant exclamation mark in the sky. The Kirti Stambh, a Jain tower of glory, predates it and is more intricate—reminding us that Chittor was not just a fortress of warriors, but of saints and scholars too.

Scattered across the plateau are palaces—of Rani Padmini, of Rana Ratan Singh—and water bodies like the Gaumukh Reservoir, which once quenched the thirst of a kingdom under siege. Temples to Meera Bai's Krishna still draw pilgrims, whispering of a different kind of love and surrender.

Today, Chittorgarh is a UNESCO World Heritage Site, and yet it feels less preserved than remembered. Tourists climb its bastions, but its true keepers are the balladeers, the folk singers, the children raised on its stories. Stories not of conquest, but of dignity in defeat. Of courage that outlived the kingdom it served.

Kumbhalgarh Fort, Rajasthan

The Fortress of the Unconquered Wall

(Rajput Consolidation 15th–17th centuries)

If Chittorgarh was the soul of Rajput sacrifice, Kumbhalgarh was its shield. Towering over the jagged hills of the Aravallis, wrapped in a serpent of stone that stretches across 36 kilometers, this was the bastion that never fell in battle. It did not host tragic *jauhars* or flaming farewells—it endured. In a land known for valiant defeats, Kumbhalgarh stood for victory by endurance.

Built in the 15th century by Rana Kumbha, the great builder-king of Mewar, Kumbhalgarh was meant as a fallback—a retreat when Chittorgarh fell, which it often did. But it was more than a military outpost. It was an act of architectural assertion. The wall of Kumbhalgarh, often called 'India's Great Wall,' is the second-longest continuous wall in the world, after China's. At its widest point, it can accommodate eight horses riding abreast. It is a marvel of medieval defense, snaking across hills and valleys like a living thing, watchful and eternal.

The fort itself is a labyrinth of bastions, gates, stepwells, and over 360 temples—both Hindu and Jain. Temples are not afterthoughts here; they are part of the fort's moral architecture. Rana Kumbha, a patron of both war and wisdom, envisioned Kumbhalgarh not just as a citadel but as a sacred refuge.

Its most famous claim to fame is as the birthplace of Maharana Pratap, the 'lion of Mewar,' born here in 1540. It was from these walls that Pratap would ride into legend, resisting Akbar's empire long after most other Rajput clans had surrendered. Kumbhalgarh, thus, is more than a fort—it is a womb of resistance, a place where legends took their first breath.

Its wall was never breached in battle. It was only conquered once, and that too through subterfuge, when the combined forces of the Mughals and allied Rajput kings briefly took it. But it was never held for long. The hills, it seemed, conspired with the defenders.

Kumbhalgarh, also a UNESCO World Heritage Site, is less frequented than Chittorgarh or Jaipur's Amber, but no less majestic. At night, the fort is illuminated, and the wall glows like a sleeping dragon—silent, but very much alive.

Jaisalmer Fort, Rajasthan

The Living Citadel of Sand and Stone

(Desert Trade and Rajput Rule 12th–18th centuries)

Jaisalmer doesn't appear—it shimmers. Rising from the shifting sands of the Thar like a dream cast in honeyed stone, the fort seems less built than conjured. And unlike most of India's great forts, Jaisalmer is still inhabited—its winding lanes echo not only with history, but with the footsteps of children, the calls of vendors, the hiss of pressure cookers.

Founded in 1156 CE by Rawal Jaisal, a Bhati Rajput ruler, the fort was built atop the Trikuta Hill to command the trade routes that linked India to Central Asia and Arabia. What it lacked in fertile surroundings, it made up for in strategy. Jaisalmer became a crucial node in the camel caravan networks, growing wealthy on the commerce of silk, spices, and stories.

Its walls, rising over 80 meters from the desert floor, are built of yellow sandstone that blazes gold at dawn and dusk, giving it the name Sonar Qila—the Golden Fort. Within its ramparts lie palaces, Jain temples, mansions (*havelis*) of merchant princes, and entire neighborhoods. Jaisalmer was never abandoned after its military relevance declined. Rather, shops moved into the bastions, guesthouses replaced watchtowers, and generations continued to be born within its walls.

Jaisalmer, too, has witnessed sieges and *jauhar*—most notably in the 13th and 14th centuries, when it fell to Alauddin Khilji's forces and later to the Sultan of Delhi. Yet it always rose again, its defenders drawn from the same sand that tried to bury them.

Architecturally, the fort is a marvel of layered life. The Raj Mahal whispers of faded grandeur, while the Jain temples are masterpieces of devotion etched in stone filigree. The intricate facades of the Patwon Ki Haveli, just outside the fort, echo the opulence of a mercantile elite that once ruled the desert as surely as any king.

Today, Jaisalmer Fort stands at a fragile intersection of heritage and habitation. Few places allow you to drink chai on a centuries-old parapet while pigeons and memory flutter around you.

Leh Palace, Ladakh

A Throne in the Clouds

(Ladakhi Kingdom 17th–19th centuries)

There are forts that command deserts, forests, and rivers. And then there is Leh Palace, perched 11,500 feet above sea level, commanding the clouds. Built not for conquest but for continuity, this humble, grey-brown structure, blending into the very rock it rests upon, is one of India's most quietly powerful citadels.

Commissioned in the 17th century by Sengge Namgyal, the most illustrious ruler of the Namgyal dynasty, Leh Palace was both a royal residence and a political nerve center for the Ladakhi kingdom. Modeled loosely on the Potala Palace of Lhasa, it was meant to assert not just authority but identity—a declaration that this Buddhist Himalayan kingdom had its own center of gravity.

Rising nine stories above the old town of Leh, the palace was more than a building. It was a world. The upper floors housed the royal family; the lower ones were for stables, servants, and storerooms. The thick earthen walls insulated against brutal winters. Narrow windows framed wide views of the Stok Kangri range and the Indus valley. In summer, the air carried the scent of juniper and barley. In winter, only the wind.

Life here was a balance of austerity and elegance. Murals adorned inner chambers. Buddhist *thangkas* and manuscripts were once housed within. Festivals and processions wove through its courtyards, mingling monastic calm with royal ceremony. But this peace was not eternal.

By the mid-19th century, as Dogra forces expanded their reach, the Namgyal dynasty fell. The royal family fled to the nearby Stok Palace, and Leh Palace was left to weather the cold alone. For over a century, it stood as a silent sentinel—roofless, empty, wind-worn.

In recent years, the Archaeological Survey of India has worked to restore parts of the palace, stabilizing walls and slowly coaxing it back to life. Today, visitors climb its worn staircases and stand on its balconies, wind in their faces, sky in their eyes. There are no golden halls here, no triumphal arches or crowded bazaars. Only silence and endurance. Leh Palace was never meant to dazzle. It was meant to last. And it has.

Bekal Fort, Kerala

The Bastion by the Sea

(Kolathiri & Nayaka Periods to Tipu Sultan 17th–19th centuries)

There are a few forts in India where the first thing you hear isn't the clatter of history but the hush of waves. At Bekal, the sea speaks before the stone does. Perched like a great sentinel on Kerala's Malabar coast, this 17th-century fort is less about royal grandeur than martial purpose. There are no darbars, no dance halls—just thick ramparts, cannon holes, and the curve of the Arabian Sea stretching to the edge of vision.

Built by Shivappa Nayaka of the Keladi Nayaka dynasty in the mid-1600s, Bekal was designed with clarity of function. This was not a courtly seat but a strategic military outpost. Its laterite walls were made to repel attack, its watchtowers to anticipate it, and its horseshoe shape—jutting boldly into the sea—offered panoramic surveillance of both coast and hinterland.

Bekal's history, like much of Kerala's coastline, is layered with power shifts. After the Nayakas, it came under the Kolathiri Rajas, then Tipu Sultan, whose reign brought Islamic influence and a strengthening of the fort's defenses. When Tipu fell in 1799, Bekal passed into British hands—absorbed into an empire that valued ports over palaces.

Unlike other forts that contain cities within walls, Bekal is almost monastic in its simplicity. A lone observation tower rises from its center, once used to station cannons and scan for enemy sails. And yet, the fort's strategic placement is timeless. Even now, one can see how its builders thought: how the walls curve with the coastline, how the water tanks are placed for siege, how the underground passage could be used for retreat. Nature and military logic work together here, not against each other.

Though Bekal has never hosted a coronation or a climactic battle, it remains one of Kerala's most visually arresting sites. It is a fort that did its job. Today, the fort is maintained by the Archaeological Survey of India and framed by palm trees, and is a favorite among picnic-goers. Its ramparts are now vantage points for sunsets, its silence punctuated by school excursions and film crews. Even so, it still watches. It always will.

Murud-Janjira, Maharashtra

The Fort That Never Surrendered

(Siddis and Maritime Resistance 15th–19th centuries)

Most forts loom above land, but Murud-Janjira rises from the sea—alone, aloof, and unyielding. Built on a rocky islet off the Konkan coast, this formidable maritime fortress remains one of India's greatest military enigmas: how did it come to be, and how did it never fall?

In the 15th century, the region was under the control of the Abyssinian Siddis of African origin who arrived in India through the ports of Gujarat and the Deccan. Serving as naval mercenaries for regional sultanates, the Siddis soon carved out autonomous power along the coast. By the late 1400s, Janjira was their stronghold—a name that derives from the Arabic *jazirah,* meaning island.

And what a stronghold it was. Encircled by high stone walls that rise sheer from the sea, equipped with bastions housing massive cannons, and accessible only by a single narrow entrance—Murud-Janjira was as impregnable as engineering allowed. It had freshwater wells inside, months of supplies, and the sea as its moat, ally, and armor.

Mughals tried to take it. The Marathas tried again and again—Shivaji, Sambhaji, even the Angres—all failed. The Portuguese tried, so did the British. All left empty-handed. At a time when naval dominance was becoming as important as land-based conquests, Janjira stood as a floating rebuke to imperial ambition.

Its 19 bastions still stand, armed with rusted but once-terrifying artillery like the Kalaal Baangdi, a cannon that once fired across the tides with legendary force. Within the walls are ruins of palaces, mosques, barracks, and hidden passages. For over 300 years, Murud-Janjira remained undefeated. The Siddis ruled from here well into the 19th century, officially under the suzerainty of the Mughals and later the British, but practically autonomous. Their unique heritage—African, Islamic, Indian—was reflected in the fort's multi-ethnic, multi-faith character.

Today, the fort can be accessed only by sailboat. Tourists walk its broken ramparts and peer through loopholes once aimed at invaders. The sea is quieter now, but the fort has not lowered its guard.

Golconda Fort, Telangana

Where Echoes Guarded Empire

(Qutb Shahi Dynasty 16th–17th centuries)

There are forts made for defense, some for display, and then there is Golconda—where architecture itself became an instrument. Built into the granite hills west of present-day Hyderabad, Golconda Fort is as famous for its acoustics as for its diamonds, as much a theatre of sound as it was a seat of power.

Originally built in the 12th century by the Kakatiya rulers of Warangal, it rose to prominence in the 16th century when the Qutb Shahi dynasty—Persianate rulers who broke away from the Bahmani Sultanate—made it their capital. What they built was a fortified city teeming with markets, mosques, palaces, baths, and the buzz of a cosmopolitan court.

At its height, Golkonda was a place of wonder. It controlled the diamond trade of the region, sourcing stones from the mines of Kollur, including the legendary Koh-i-Noor and Hope diamonds. Merchants came from Persia, Arabia, and Europe. Poets composed in Persian and Dakhni Urdu. Sultans held court in halls of stucco and lime, under domes that caught the breeze of the Deccan.

The fort itself sprawls across several kilometers of hill and plain, rising from a bustling lower city to a citadel atop a 400-foot-high granite outcrop. Its strategic brilliance lies in its layered defenses—gates angled to repel elephants, walls that absorb impact, and a series of acoustic marvels that acted as early warning systems. A clap at the main Fateh Darwaza can be heard clearly atop the citadel, a kilometer away—a signal for guards, a deterrent to spies, a marvel to tourists today.

Golkonda's golden age ended in 1687 when Aurangzeb laid siege to the fort for eight months. The gates eventually opened—some say by betrayal, others by brute force. Today, Golconda Fort is both a ruin and a wonder. Its walls are fractured, its palaces empty, but its grandeur persists. Climb to the summit, and the city of Hyderabad stretches before you—a testament to the ambition and artistry that once echoed from these stones.

Rajgad Fort, Maharashtra

The Cradle of the Maratha Empire

(Shivaji Maharaj's Reign, 17th century)

Not all capitals are built in cities. Some are raised in the clouds. Rajgad, the 'King of Forts,' rises from the Western Ghats like a coiled cobra—serene in appearance, lethal when provoked. For 26 years, this was the nerve center of one of the most remarkable military and administrative revolutions in Indian history: the rise of Chhatrapati Shivaji Maharaj and the birth of Hindavi Swarajya.

Originally known as Murumbdev, the fort was captured by Shivaji Maharaj in 1648 and transformed into his first capital. It was from here that he laid the foundations of a kingdom built on mobility, terrain mastery, and the decentralized strength of hill forts. If Raigad would later become the ceremonial capital, Rajgad remained his crucible—where strategies were tested, treaties written, and loyalty forged in steel.

Perched at over 4,300 feet above sea level, Rajgad is not a single structure but a natural fortress with a brilliant man-made core. The fort is divided into three sprawling spurs—Padmavati Machi (the residential and administrative complex), Suvela Machi (the eastern defensive wing), and Sanjeevani Machi (a long, narrow projection built for layered fortification). At its center rises the Balekilla, the citadel, where Shivaji Maharaj's private quarters once stood—commanding views of endless valleys and, on clear days, other forts in the Maratha network.

Rajgad saw not just governance but pivotal events in Shivaji Maharaj's life. His mother, Jijabai, spent her final years here. It was here that he planned his daring raid on Shaista Khan in Pune. His son, Rajaram, was born within these walls. And from these very ramparts, he later moved to Raigad, confident that the foundation had been laid.

The fort's architecture is not about ornament—it is about resilience. Steep approaches, hidden gates, water cisterns dug into rock, and observation points perfectly aligned with enemy paths. It was built to survive, and it did. Today, Rajgad is a pilgrimage site for trekkers and patriots alike. The climb is demanding, the weather unpredictable, but the reward is unchanging: the wind, the view, and the sense that atop this rugged peak, an empire once dreamed—and dared.

Raigad Fort, Maharashtra

Where Swarajya Wore a Crown

(Coronation of Shivaji Maharaj and Maratha Rule, 17th century)

High above the Konkan plains, at 2851 feet above sea level, Raigad rises out of the mist like a judgment shaped by basalt and the will of a man who believed that power could be born from the people and shaped in the hills. This was not a fort built for a king—it was where a man became one.

Captured by Shivaji Maharaj from the local More rulers in 1656, Raigad was strategically chosen for its near-impenetrable location and commanding views. Over the next decade, it was transformed into a full-fledged capital—complete with palaces, granaries, market avenues, assembly halls, and even a mint. In 1674, after years of guerrilla warfare, political maneuvering, and relentless vision, Shivaji Maharaj was crowned Chhatrapati of the Maratha Empire on these very heights. The coronation was not just ceremonial. It was ideological. It asserted, for the first time in centuries, an indigenous Hindu kingship in a land long ruled by sultans and emperors.

The fort's design reflects this mix of ambition and pragmatism. The Mena Darwaza—a private entrance used by royal women—leads to the Queen's quarters. The Nagarkhana Darwaza opens into the main public square where the Raj Sabha once echoed with statecraft. In front stands the Takht, the throne platform, where Shivaji Maharaj would sit—his back to the Sahyadris, his gaze fixed on his ministers, his people, and his dream.

Nearby lies Jagadishwar Mandir, the king's private place of worship, and not far from it, Shivaji Maharaj's tomb—a simple, stone structure marked by an eternal flame and the statue of his loyal dog, Waghya, who is said to have leapt into his master's pyre. He passed away here in 1680, at just 50, leaving behind not just a fort, but a flame of resistance that continued to burn across generations.

Raigad fell to the Mughals after Shivaji Maharaj's death, was retaken by the Marathas, and was captured by the British in 1818. To this day, it remains a site of pilgrimage for anyone who wishes to stand at the birthplace of a radical Indian idea: that self-rule was not a dream but a duty.

Shivneri Fort, Maharashtra

Where a King Was Born

(Birthplace of Shivaji Maharaj, 17th century)

In a quiet corner of the Sahyadris, near the town of Junnar, a fort rises—compact, austere, and unpretentious. It lacks the scale of Raigad, the drama of Rajgad, or the audacity of Janjira. But it holds something rarer: origin. On this hill, in 1630, Jijabai gave birth to a child named Shivaji—a name that would become a movement, a vision, a battle cry.

Shivneri Fort predates Shivaji Maharaj by centuries. It was once a stronghold during the Satavahana period and later came under Yadava, Bahmani, and eventually Ahmadnagar rule. In the early 17th century, the fort was under the control of the Mughals, but Shahaji Raje, Shivaji Maharaj's father and a Maratha commander in their service, ensured that his wife resided safely here during her pregnancy. It was a decision less military than maternal—and yet, as history unfolded, it came to seem prophetic.

Perched on a triangular hill, with steep rock faces and a commanding view of the plains below, Shivneri was ideal for protection. Seven gates lead up to the main complex—each designed to slow an enemy and buy time for defense. Within the fort lies the modest Shiv Janmasthan, the chamber traditionally believed to be Shivaji Maharaj's birthplace. Nearby, the Badami Talav, a central water tank, still collects monsoon rain, reflecting the same sky the infant warrior once gazed up at.

One of the fort's most striking features is its simplicity. It was not a capital, nor a court. It was a womb of stone—secure, silent, watchful. Yet from its quiet walls emerged a child who would go on to challenge the most powerful empire in the subcontinent, and whose name would be remembered centuries later as a symbol of resistance and self-rule.

Visitors today ascend the fort via a well-trodden path flanked by greenery in the monsoon and golden scrub in the summer. Along the way are memorials, cannons, and views that stretch far into the Deccan. The air feels different here—not because of altitude, but because of what began. If Raigad is where the Maratha dream reached its zenith, Shivneri is where it opened its eyes.

Sinhagad Fort, Maharashtra

Where the Lion Laid Down His Life

(Maratha Resistance, 17th–18th centuries)

Some forts are remembered for what they protected. Sinhagad is remembered for what it cost. Perched atop a cliff southwest of Pune, Sinhagad is a fortress not of monuments but of memory. The Marathas called it Sinhagad: the Lion's Fort. And they meant it literally.

Known as Kondhana in earlier times, and predating Shivaji Maharaj by centuries, it was strategically placed to control trade routes and access into the Pune plateau. Its steep slopes, narrow paths, and fortified gates made it nearly impregnable. But it became truly legendary in 1670, when Chhatrapati Shivaji Maharaj sought to recapture it from the Mughals—and chose Tanaji Malusare, his most trusted commander, to lead the charge.

Tanaji, it is said, was preparing for his son's wedding when he received the summons. He left immediately, telling his family, 'First the fort, then the festivities.' What followed was one of the most daring night assaults in Indian military history. Tanaji and his men scaled the steep cliff using a monitor lizard named Yashwanti, whose claws gripped the rock face as a rope was tied to her. The Marathas clambered up in the dead of night and launched a brutal attack.

Victory came—but at a price. Tanaji was killed in combat. When Shivaji heard the news, he is said to have wept, uttering the immortal words: *'Gad aala pan sinha gela'*—'The fort is won, but the lion is lost.' The fort was renamed Sinhagad in Tanaji's honor.

Sinhagad would change hands several times between the Marathas and the Mughals before finally being secured by the former under Peshwa rule. During the British era, it served briefly as a garrison, and later became a site of nationalist pilgrimage. Even Mahatma Gandhi's son was once imprisoned here. The fort has two main gates—Kalyan Darwaza and Pune Darwaza—that lead to a series of open spaces, temples, granaries, and watch points. The wind is constant, and the views are vast. Today, Sinhagad is a popular trekking destination, and at the top, a simple samadhi marks the place where Tanaji fell.

Vijayadurg Fort, Maharashtra

The Ocean's Strongest Citadel

(Maratha Naval Power, 17th–18th centuries)

Vijayadurg commands the sea. Built originally by the rulers of the Shilahar dynasty and expanded in the 17th century by Shivaji Maharaj, it became one of the most impregnable naval fortresses in Indian history. Located on a narrow creek that cuts into the Konkan coast, the fort was perfectly positioned to defend against sea invasions, control trade routes, and launch maritime operations. This was no outpost—it was a headquarters.

Shivaji Maharaj, the visionary warrior-king, understood that empire wasn't just land—it was water. And to rule the western coastline, he needed more than horses and hills. He needed harbors, docks, ships, and commanders who knew the sea like the back of their sword hands. Under his reign, Vijayadurg evolved into a naval shipyard and a fortress equipped with high bastions, massive cannons, and defenses that anticipated both storm and siege.

Unlike many coastal forts, Vijayadurg is built of solid laterite stone and stretches deep into the sea itself—at high tide, it appears as though the waves part around it. The outer walls are triple-layered, and secret underwater trenches made it impossible for enemy ships to approach unchallenged. At one point, a 200-meter undersea chain was believed to block unwanted vessels.

It wasn't just a Maratha pride—it was their sea lion. Kanhoji Angre, Shivaji Maharaj's legendary admiral, used Vijayadurg as his naval base, harassing European ships and asserting Indian maritime sovereignty in an age dominated by colonial navies. The fort held its own against the British, the Dutch, and the Portuguese—its cannons speaking the language of resistance far beyond the land-bound empire.

Eventually, in 1818, as part of the fall of the Maratha confederacy, Vijayadurg was captured by the British. But its maritime legacy remained unmatched.

Today, the fort is battered but formidable. Visitors walk along walls where lookouts once scanned for sails, and they listen to the ocean—whose voice still seems to echo with the orders of commanders, the creak of oars, and the dignity of a people who dared to dream beyond the shore.

Bidar Fort, Karnataka

Where the Deccan Found Its Voice

(Bahmani and Barid Shahi Sultanates, 15th–17th centuries)

Atop a laterite plateau in northern Karnataka, surrounded by the dusty hues of the Deccan, lies Bidar Fort—a place less famous than it deserves, yet one of the most eloquent voices in the long conversation of Indian architecture. It is not just a fort. It is a sultanate's diary—written in domes, corridors, battlements, and glazed tiles.

The original fortification at Bidar dates back to the 8th century, but its true transformation came in 1429, when Sultan Ahmad Shah Wali of the Bahmani dynasty shifted the capital from Gulbarga to Bidar. What followed was a frenzy of building—mosques, palaces, gardens, madrasas, and gateways—designed to turn a hilltop into a court of ideas and power. Persian artisans were invited, Deccani masters employed, and a new vocabulary of Indo-Islamic style took form.

The fort's outer walls stretch nearly two kilometers, reinforced by 37 bastions and a wide moat. But its brilliance lies within. The Rangin Mahal, with its vividly colored tilework and intricately carved wood, remains a masterpiece of aesthetic ambition. The Gagan Mahal, Tarkash Mahal, and Solah Khamba Mosque reveal an architectural confidence both eclectic and elegant—merging Persian motifs with Deccan materials and techniques.

Perhaps the most remarkable institution within the fort was the Madrasa of Mahmud Gawan, built by a Persian merchant-scholar who rose to become prime minister of the Bahmani state. The madrasa was more than an educational center—it was a symbol of what the Deccan could be: inclusive, intellectual, and interconnected with the Islamic world. Though now partially in ruins, its tiled minarets and austere grace still inspire awe.

After the fall of the Bahmanis, Bidar passed into the hands of the Barid Shahi dynasty and later became a strategic outpost for the Mughals and the Hyderabad Nizams. But none replicated its cultural flourish.

Today, Bidar Fort is less crowded than it should be. Restoration work is ongoing, and visitors can wander through palace ruins and down arched corridors where the air still carries echoes of Persian couplets and Deccani debates.

Jhansi Fort, Uttar Pradesh

Where a Queen Stood and Never Fell

(Bundela Dynasty to 1857 Rebellion, 18th–19th centuries)

There are forts that house kings, and there are forts that forge legends. Jhansi is the latter. Rising from a granite outcrop in the heart of Bundelkhand, it is not the most ornate, the tallest, or the largest—but it may be the most loved. Because in 1857, amid betrayal, bombardment, and impossible odds, a young widow-turned-queen stood her ground here—and made history burn brighter.

Originally built by Raja Bir Singh Deo of Orchha in the early 17th century, Jhansi Fort changed hands through the Marathas and eventually became the seat of Rani Lakshmibai, the queen who would become a symbol of resistance in the First War of Indian Independence. When her adopted son was denied succession by the British under the Doctrine of Lapse, and Jhansi was annexed, she did not bow—she braced.

In 1857, as the rebellion flared across north India, Lakshmibai fortified the fort, trained soldiers, forged alliances, and refused to surrender. British troops laid siege for weeks. Cannons thundered, walls cracked, and fire rained down—but the queen held firm. It is said that when defeat became inevitable, she tied her infant son to her back, mounted her horse, and leapt from the fort's ramparts into history. She fought, regrouped, and died in battle shortly after—but never in surrender.

The fort itself is built for functionality—thick walls, deep ditches, and a commanding view of the plains below. It covers nearly 15 acres and contains within it the Rani Mahal, military barracks, temples, and water reservoirs that sustained it through sieges. The famous Jumping Point—where the queen is said to have leapt—is now a place of pilgrimage, draped in reverence rather than ruin.

Jhansi Fort has no gilded chambers or carved balconies. Its beauty is its courage, its claim to immortality is forged not in gold but in grit. Every child who visits learns her name. Every textbook tells her tale. And every Independence Day, she rides again—in the imagination of a country that still believes in bravery without compromise.

Diu Fort, Daman and Diu

Portugal's Last Watchtower

(Portuguese Colonial Period, 16th–20th centuries)

At the edge of Gujarat's Kathiawar coast, the Arabian Sea crashes endlessly against the thick ramparts of Diu Fort. For over four centuries, it was not India that stood here—but Portugal. A sentinel of an empire, a gateway to the East, and ultimately, a relic of Europe's longest colonial holdout on Indian soil.

Built in 1535 after the Portuguese secured the island of Diu through a strategic alliance with Sultan Bahadur Shah of Gujarat, the fort was a response to growing threats from Ottoman naval forces and the rising ambitions of other European powers. It was a statement that Portugal, though small in size, would cast a long shadow.

The result was formidable: a massive bastion surrounded on three sides by water, equipped with double moats, thick embankments, and strategically positioned bastions like Panikhota (a detached sea fortification) that turned Diu into a floating fortress. The armory was stocked with bronze cannons from Europe, some of which remain rusting but resolute along the parapets.

Within the walls, a small colonial world unfolded—churches, barracks, a lighthouse, a prison, and supply warehouses. Catholic crosses sat uneasily beside Islamic inscriptions, and sea breezes whispered in Konkani, Gujarati, and Portuguese. For nearly 400 years, Diu remained a Portuguese possession—even as other European powers were swept away, and the Indian mainland changed rulers and empires.

It wasn't until 1961—14 years after Indian independence—that Diu, along with Daman and Goa, was annexed by India in a brief military operation. The fort, by then outdated and ceremonial, stood by silently as the last Portuguese tricolor was lowered.

Today, the fort endures as a hauntingly intact structure, maintained by the Archaeological Survey of India. Visitors walk its ramparts and peer through cannon holes, no longer pointed at invaders but at fishing boats and tourist ferries. Inside the old prison, voices echo. Outside, gulls circle overhead like watchmen who never left. Diu Fort may no longer guard an empire, but it reminds us of how long empires can linger—quiet, weathered, watching the sea.

Daulatabad Fort, Maharashtra

The Fortress of Foolish Glory

(Yadava Dynasty to Tughlaq Era, 12th–14th centuries)

Few forts in India rise with the drama of Daulatabad. Perched atop a conical hill of black basalt, it is not merely built—it is embedded into the earth. But what truly makes Daulatabad legendary is the imperial folly that once tried to make this place the capital of all Hindustan.

Originally known as Devagiri, the fort was founded in the 12th century by the Yadava kings of the Deccan. It rose to prominence as a regional power center—strategically located on the trade routes between north and south India, surrounded by fertile plains, and nearly impregnable in design. Its defenses were layered: a complex series of moats, drawbridges, false doors, steep staircases, and a dark, bat-filled tunnel designed to mislead invaders.

But Daulatabad's moment of national infamy came in the 14th century, when Delhi Sultan Muhammad bin Tughlaq, in a burst of strategic megalomania, decided to shift his capital, in 1327, from Delhi to this remote fortress nearly a thousand kilometers away. Tughlak renamed the fort from Devagiri to Daulatabad. He ordered the entire court, administration, and even population to march south. The result was chaos. Disease, dislocation, and despair followed. Within a few years, the capital was returned to Delhi—but Daulatabad's myth was sealed.

Despite this misstep, the fort continued to serve various rulers. The Bahmani Sultans, the Nizam Shahis of Ahmednagar, the Mughals, and eventually the Hyderabad Nizams all held it at various times. Its value was always the same: near-inaccessibility. The final ascent to the topmost citadel, through a pitch-dark passage known as the Andheri, remains one of the most daunting defensive designs in any fort in India.

From the summit, the view is a panoramic sweep of the Deccan, dotted with water tanks, mosques, and remains of once-grand halls. The Chand Minar, a 30-meter-high tower built in the 15th century, stands like a sentinel, its Persian-style stucco still bearing traces of blue. Today, Daulatabad is a dramatic ruin. Tourists explore its twisted staircases and whisper in its dark tunnels. It no longer guards a kingdom, but it guards a story: of hubris, grandeur, and the sheer audacity of thinking that geography could be destiny.

Uparkot Fort, Gujarat

The Fort That Watched Time Flow

(Mauryan to Solanki Periods, 3rd century BCE–15th century CE)

In Junagadh, time is not linear—it's layered. And nowhere is that layering more vivid than at Uparkot Fort, where kings and monks, sultans and saints, all left their mark upon the same rock. This is not a fort in the conventional sense. It is a living excavation site, a museum without walls, a city upon a city.

Perched on a plateau at the eastern edge of Junagadh, Uparkot is believed to have been originally fortified in the 3rd century BCE during the Mauryan period. Nearby, Ashoka's rock edicts still proclaim tolerance and dharma to all who can still read the ancient Brahmi script. Beneath the fort lie the Buddhist caves—rock-cut chambers with pillared halls and stone benches, echoing with a silence that dates back over two thousand years. Monks once meditated here; tourists now marvel at their restraint and geometry.

The fort's name, Uparkot, means 'upper citadel,' and for centuries, it served as the stronghold of the rulers of this region—whether Hindu, Muslim, or Jain. The fort was rebuilt and expanded during the Gupta, Maitraka, Chudasama, and later Solanki dynasties. It was said to have withstood sieges lasting years, thanks to its ingenious water systems: deep wells like the Adi Kadi Vav and Navghan Kuvo, which plunge straight into the earth, ensuring that the fort never goes thirsty, even if it is starving.

Architecturally, Uparkot is a curious, compelling mix. Its walls are massive—20 feet thick in places—and its gates are adorned with Indo-Saracenic flourishes added later during Islamic rule. Inside lie palace ruins, cannon placements (including the famed Neelam and Manek, brought by Turks), and scattered reminders of its many phases of occupation.

The old city of Junagadh still curls around it. Devotees on pilgrimage to Mount Girnar pass by its base. Langurs perch on its ramparts, and kids play cricket in its courtyards. All the while, beneath their feet, rest layers of India's civilizational sediment. To visit Uparkot is to walk through time, one era at a time.

Gwalior Fort, Madhya Pradesh

The Gibraltar of India

(From Tomar to Mughal to Scindia Rule, 10th–20th centuries)

To stand on the walls of Gwalior Fort is to stand at a crossroads—where legend meets politics, where artistry meets violence, and where power constantly changed hands, but never left the hill. Spread over a massive sandstone outcrop in the heart of Madhya Pradesh, Gwalior has been called 'the Gibraltar of India' for good reason: it was nearly unconquerable, and never unimportant.

The origins of the fort are lost in time, though it finds early mention as far back as the 6th century. Its golden age, however, begins in the 9th and 10th centuries, with the Kachchhapaghatas and later the Tomars—most notably Raja Man Singh Tomar in the 15th century. It was he who transformed Gwalior from a garrison into a palace of dreams.

Man Singh built the famed Man Mandir Palace, whose façade of glazed blue tiles and delicate stone latticework still stuns the eye. Inside, mirrored ceilings, acoustically perfect music halls, and labyrinthine corridors spoke not just of wealth, but refinement. It is said that Tansen—the great musician of Akbar's court—trained here. If the hills had ears, this is where they first heard ragas.

But the fort was no idle pleasure dome. It was strategic, towering 300 feet above the surrounding plain, with cliffs on every side. It passed from Tomars to Mughals, from Marathas to the British, and finally to the Scindias—each leaving behind inscriptions, tombs, and scars. Babur called it 'the pearl among fortresses.' Aurangzeb used it to imprison and execute his brother Murad. Rani Laxmibai sought refuge here after the fall of Jhansi, only to die nearby in the battle of Kotah Ki Serai.

Within its sprawling precincts lie Jain rock-cut sculptures, ancient temples like the Teli Ka Mandir and Sas-Bahu, British-era barracks, and underground prisons. Today, Gwalior Fort is a heritage site, a stage for music festivals, and a symbol of the city's identity. The sounds of gunfire have long faded, replaced now by strains of classical ragas that rise, fittingly, from Tansen's tomb nearby.

Chitradurga Fort, Karnataka

The Fort of Stone and Storm

(Nayakas of Chitradurga and Mysore Kingdom, 15th–18th centuries)

There are some forts in India where the terrain seems to have declared war—and then decided to join the defenders. Chitradurga, in central Karnataka, is not merely built atop hills, it is the hills. Massive granite boulders, windswept ridges, and irregular outcrops shape the fort's form as much as any human hand. This is a citadel of camouflage and cunning, of raw stone and resistance.

The origins of Chitradurga stretch back to antiquity—traces of Neolithic life have been found in nearby caves—but its strategic importance crystallized under the Nayakas of Chitradurga, a local dynasty that ruled from the 15th to 18th centuries under the Vijayanagara Empire and later independently. Over generations, they expanded and fortified the hills, eventually creating a seven-tiered defensive marvel known locally as Yelu Suttina Kote—the fort of seven encirclements.

Each wall was a threshold, each gate, a puzzle. The entrances were deliberately narrow and twisting to prevent elephant charges. Watchtowers were carved into boulders. Secret passages, granaries, and water tanks were cleverly hidden in plain sight. At the summit stood the main citadel, commanding a sweeping view of the plains and approaching armies.

The fort saw many sieges, but none as famous as the attack by Hyder Ali in the late 18th century. Legend has it that when Hyder's forces found a small crevice through which they intended to breach the fort, a woman named Onake Obavva, the wife of a watchman, discovered them. Armed with just an *onake* (a pestle), she struck down enemy soldiers one by one as they crept through the opening, buying precious time before reinforcements arrived. Today, the spot is known as Obavvana Kindi, and she is a folk heroine across Karnataka.

Eventually, Chitradurga fell to Hyder Ali, and later passed to the British. But it was never truly defeated. It still stands—rugged, stoic, scarred by cannon fire. Today, visitors climb its uneven paths and are awed by the fort's complexity and raw aesthetic. This is not architecture. It is survival, sculpted.

Fort St. George, Tamil Nadu

Where the Empire Came Ashore

(British East India Company, 17th–19th centuries)

In the heart of Chennai, amid government buildings and colonial echoes, stands a fortress that began not as a bastion of war, but of trade. Fort St. George, established in 1644 by the British East India Company, was the first British fortress in India—and the first brick in an empire that would grow, over centuries, into domination.

When the British arrived on the southeastern coast, they weren't seeking to rule, but to profit. Spices, cloth, indigo, and influence were the cargo. A small strip of land was leased from the local Nayaka rulers, and here the Company built a fortified trading post. It was named after St. George, the patron saint of England, and quickly became the nucleus around which the city of Madras (now Chennai) would grow.

At first glance, Fort St. George lacks drama—it is flat, functional, and restrained—its architecture more suited to ledgers than legends. But within its barracks and corridors, treaties were signed, wars were planned, and policies were drawn up that would reshape the entire subcontinent. The fort housed everything: administrative offices, warehouses, residences, and barracks. It also contained the oldest Anglican church in India—St. Mary's Church, consecrated in 1680. It was here that Robert Clive, the future architect of British India, was married. Outside the church stands the oldest British tombstone in the country, dated 1661.

Over time, Fort St. George weathered sieges and storms. It was briefly captured by the French in the mid-18th century but was soon retaken. As British power expanded, the fort became the seat of the Madras Presidency, one of the three major administrative divisions of British India. Decisions made here would ripple across villages, provinces, and generations.

Today, Fort St. George is still in use. It houses the Tamil Nadu Legislative Assembly and Secretariat, making it one of the rare forts in India still performing a form of governance. Its museum, with faded portraits, colonial furniture, and Company artefacts, tells a story that is both proud and painful. To walk through Fort St. George is to walk through the prologue of the British Raj.

Fort William, West Bengal

The Bastion of British Bengal

(East India Company to British Raj, 18th–20th centuries)

It began as a trade outpost, became a fortress, then a seat of government, and finally, the headquarters of an empire. Fort William, built on the eastern banks of the Hooghly River in what would become the city of Kolkata, was not constructed to inspire. But in its squat geometry and martial confidence, it became the backbone of British Bengal and a symbol of colonial permanence.

The first Fort William was completed in 1706 by the British East India Company, and was named after King William III. It was modest in scope, intended to defend a growing trading community against European rivals and Indian powers alike. But in 1756, when Nawab Siraj-ud-Daulah of Bengal attacked and briefly seized the fort, it led to an episode that would pass into infamy: the Black Hole of Calcutta. As legend had it, dozens of British prisoners were confined overnight in a small room, with only a handful surviving. The tale—true or embellished—became a rallying cry in London for revenge and re-conquest.

The response came swiftly. After Robert Clive's victory at the Battle of Plassey in 1757, the East India Company secured not just Fort William, but the entirety of Bengal. A new, far more massive fort was constructed—completed by 1781—south of the original site. This second Fort William was a military city unto itself, covering 70 acres, surrounded by a moat, and equipped with enormous open fields (the Maidan) to ensure clear lines of fire.

The fort never again saw a serious assault. Instead, it served as the Eastern Command headquarters, housing thousands of British troops. It was from here that Bengal was administered, rebellions monitored, and resources extracted. As Kolkata grew into the capital of British India, Fort William stood as a nerve center of colonial authority.

Fort William is still a functioning military base, under the Indian Army's Eastern Command. Public access is restricted, but its presence looms over the heart of the city. In a city of art, poetry, and revolution, Fort William remains a paradox—an island of unyielding discipline surrounded by a sea of voices that once rose against it.

Amber Fort, Rajasthan

Where the Walls Were Woven in Light

(Kachhwaha Dynasty and Mughal Era 16th–18th centuries)

Rising from the Aravalli hills just outside Jaipur, Amber Fort's honey-hued façade reflects not just sunlight, but centuries of architectural dialog between Rajput chivalry and Mughal finesse.

In the 10th century, the Meena tribes first fortified the hill of Amber. By the late 16th century, Raja Man Singh I, trusted general of Akbar and scion of the Kachhwaha Rajputs, began building the fort that would become a fusion of battlefield awareness and courtly refinement. Successive rulers, especially Mirza Raja Jai Singh and Sawai Jai Singh II, expanded it, turning the structure into a series of interlinked palaces, temples, and gardens cascading down the hill. Amber is entered with a climb—past cobbled paths and elephant processions, past the Suraj Pol (Sun Gate), into a world that feels both ancient and enchanted. The Jaleb Chowk, where armies once assembled, leads to the Diwan-i-Aam, a pillared hall open to the elements, and beyond it lie the heartbeats of Amber: the Sheesh Mahal, the Hall of Mirrors, where a single lamp could multiply into a constellation; the Sukh Niwas, where cool air once flowed over water channels and sandalwood doors; and the Zenana, a maze of chambers and latticework designed for privacy and intrigue.

For all its beauty, Amber Fort was not merely a palace, but a strategic marvel. Its walls wrapped around the surrounding hills, concealing passages, guard posts, and escape routes leading to the more austere Jaigarh Fort above—a silent sentinel overlooking the ornamental joy below. Together, they formed a twin system of protection and performance.

Amber's significance extended beyond its architecture. The Kachhwahas, unlike some other Rajput clans, allied early with the Mughals, marrying into the imperial family and exchanging martial valor for political stability. As a result, Amber became a place of cultural synthesis—where Persian paintings met Rajasthani miniatures, and Mughal gardens bloomed beside Rajput courtyards.

Today, Amber Fort is one of India's most visited monuments, a UNESCO World Heritage Site, and a symbol of the Jaipur aesthetic. By day, its halls echo with tourists' footsteps. By night, its walls glow under light-and-sound shows that whisper legends into the wind.

Nahargarh Fort, Rajasthan

The Quiet Sentinel of the Pink City

(Kachhwaha Rule under Sawai Jai Singh II (18th–19th centuries)

Nahargarh Fort was built for perspective. Perched high on the Aravalli Hills to the north of Jaipur, its purpose was never to wage wars but to witness—and to whisper warnings if the horizon ever changed.

Commissioned in 1734 by Maharaja Sawai Jai Singh II, the visionary founder of Jaipur, Nahargarh was part of a defensive trio, along with Jaigarh and Amber, meant to guard the new capital from the north. Its name means 'Abode of Tigers,' though legend offers a more spectral explanation: that the fort was haunted by the spirit of a Rathore prince named Nahar Singh Bhomia, whose restless soul was only appeased after a shrine was built in his honor on the site. Hence—Nahargarh.

Unlike its more martial cousins, Nahargarh never saw a major battle. Instead, it became a place of retreat, strategy, and silent watching. From its ramparts, Jaipur unfolds below like a painted scroll—its gridded avenues, domes, and bazaars softened by distance. And within its walls, the royals of Jaipur built for comfort, not campaign.

The fort's most exquisite section is the Madhavendra Bhawan, built in the 19th century by Sawai Ram Singh II. It is a two-story pleasure palace with a twist: twelve identical suites for the twelve queens, all connected by corridors that led to the king's central quarters. The design was clever, elegant, and discreet. Each suite was adorned with delicate frescoes, *jharokhas,* and colored glass, offering privacy without distance.

Nahargarh's significance grew with time. During the 1857 uprising, the fort sheltered European families evacuated from Jaipur. In the 20th century, it served briefly as a hunting lodge, then as a government office. Today, Nahargarh is one of Jaipur's most beloved landmarks. By day, tourists climb its bastions and trace the skyline with their fingers. By night, the city lights below twinkle like offerings to a patient sentinel. The fort has also made cinematic appearances—most memorably in *Rang De Basanti,* where its ramparts framed revolution and reckoning. Nahargarh is a place of vantage. A fort not to conquer—but to understand.

Chauragarh Fort, Madhya Pradesh

The Watchtower of Gondwana

(Gond Dynasty, 16th–18th centuries)

Chauragarh does not appear suddenly. It reveals itself slowly—first as a glint of stone through teak forests, then as steps carved into the rock, and finally as a windswept summit wrapped in ritual and memory.

Located in the Pachmarhi region of the Satpura range, Chauragarh was once a bastion of the Gond rulers, the indigenous dynasty that controlled vast swathes of central India from the 14th to 18th centuries. At its height, Gondwana was not a backwater—it was a sophisticated federation of tribal polities, each ruled by kings and queens who held court in forts like Garha, Mandla, and here, at Chauragarh.

It was in the 16th century that Chauragarh rose to prominence under King Sangram Shah of Garha-Mandla, who is said to have fortified the hill as a defensive outpost and religious site. But its most stirring chapter came later, during the reign of Rani Durgavati, his daughter-in-law and one of India's few remembered warrior queens.

When the Mughals advanced under Asaf Khan in 1564, Durgavati refused to surrender. She led her armies on horseback, bow in hand, into the thick forests and rolling hills of Gondwana. Her final stand came not far from Chauragarh. Wounded and unwilling to be captured, she took her own life. Chauragarh, some say, was her last stronghold—the watchtower that bore witness as resistance turned to legend.

The fort is accessed by a grueling stairway of more than 1,300 steps—each one ascending deeper into silence and sky. At the summit stands not a palace, but a Shiva temple, adorned with thousands of tridents (*trishuls*) left by pilgrims over centuries. The fort's original structures are largely in ruins—moss-covered walls, a few bastions, and broken stone platforms—but the soul of the place remains intact.

Chauragarh today is less a fort and more a pilgrimage site, especially during Mahashivratri, when devotees climb the steps bearing tridents as offerings. The military function has long faded, but the spiritual charge is potent. The Gonds are no longer rulers, but their memories still rule the land.

Vasai Fort, Maharashtra

The Forgotten Fortress of Conquest and Cross

(Portuguese and Maratha Eras, 16th–18th centuries)

Travel north from Mumbai, past the urban sprawl and salt flats, and you will reach Vasai—an unassuming coastal town where vines curl through broken cloisters and birds nest in baroque arches. Few realize that this is the site of one of the most significant European strongholds ever built in India. This is Bassein, as the Portuguese called it. This is Vasai Fort.

In the 16th century, as Portuguese power grew along India's western coast, the crown sought to expand its influence beyond Goa. Bassein, then a minor port under Gujarat's sultans, was strategically ideal—close to the lucrative northern trade routes, yet shielded by creeks and marshes. In 1534, the Treaty of Bassein ceded the region to the Portuguese, and what followed was a transformation.

They built not a fort, but a fortified city. Sprawling over 110 acres, Vasai Fort included churches, seminaries, houses, markets, and a cathedral. High stone walls were reinforced with bastions and artillery emplacements. Watchtowers scanned the sea. Cannons faced both the water and the land. And inside, the cross stood tall. For over two centuries, Vasai was the heart of northern Portuguese India—more important than Bombay, more fortified than Diu. Jesuit missionaries launched their spiritual campaigns from here. Trade flowed—spices, horses, textiles, even slaves. The architecture fused European styles with local stone. Façades bore Portuguese coats of arms. Yet beneath the European veneer, the rhythms of India endured.

But no fort is eternal. In 1739, Chimaji Appa, brother of the Maratha Peshwa Baji Rao I, laid siege to Vasai. The Marathas knew the fort's strengths, but also its weaknesses. After months of battle and blockade, the Portuguese capitulated. The cross gave way to the *bhagwa dhwaj*, the saffron flag. It was one of the greatest Maratha victories against European colonizers. In the British period, Vasai lost its prominence. Bombay rose. Bassein fell silent.

Today, Vasai Fort is a beautiful ruin, overgrown yet awe-inspiring. The sea laps gently at its mossy ramparts, and the skeletal remains of churches stand against the sky like forgotten prayers.

Kangra Fort, Himachal Pradesh

The Fort That Refused to Forget

(Trigarta Kingdom to Katoch Dynasty, Ancient–19th century)

Nestled against the Dhauladhar range, Kangra Fort is India's oldest dated fort—referenced as far back as the Mahabharata, and later mentioned in the chronicles of Alexander the Great. And yet, for all its age and erosion, its heart remains intact.

The fort stands on a strategic hilltop above the confluence of two rivers, a natural moat that made it almost impregnable. The region, known in ancient times as Trigarta, was ruled for centuries by the Katoch dynasty—one of India's oldest royal lineages. Kangra was their pride, their center of power, and their deepest scar.

It was coveted endlessly. Mahmud of Ghazni plundered it in 1009 CE—drawn by its legendary treasure-laden temples, especially the nearby Brijeshwari Devi Mandir. He broke the fort, but not the dynasty. Others followed: Firoz Shah Tughlaq in the 14th century, Sher Shah Suri in the 16th, and even the Mughals, who finally captured it under Akbar. Yet each time, the Katochs returned—sometimes as rulers, sometimes as rebels, but always as rightful heirs.

Architecturally, Kangra Fort reflects its long, layered past. Its massive stone walls snake up the hill, punctuated by lofty gates—Ranjit Singh Darwaza, Jehangiri Darwaza, Andheri Darwaza. Within the walls lie ruins of palaces, temples, and a stepwell that still holds rainwater. The views from the top—snow peaks in the distance, river valleys below—remind you why so many came to claim it. In the 18th century, Raja Sansar Chand, a Katoch visionary and patron of the arts, reclaimed Kangra and made it a cultural hub. But in 1809, the fort was lost to Maharaja Ranjit Singh of Punjab. Later, the British annexed it after the Anglo-Sikh wars. In 1905, a devastating earthquake ravaged the fort, toppling walls and towers, and silencing what remained of its political relevance.

Even in ruin, Kangra breathes. Pilgrims still climb its ramparts. And the Katoch name still resonates in the valleys—more myth than monarchy now, but no less powerful. Today, the fort is managed by the Archaeological Survey of India, and efforts are underway to preserve what remains. But Kangra asks only to be remembered.

Qila Mubarak (Bathinda Fort), Punjab

The Tallest Memory of the North

(Kushan to Mughal Era, 1st–18th centuries)

Rising from the plains of Bathinda like a great, earthen tower, this fort is one of India's oldest surviving structures in continuous use. Built originally during the Kushan period—some say as early as the 1st century CE—it predates many of the dynasties that later ruled from its ramparts. And yet it still stands, solemn and dignified, the grandfather of northern citadels.

The fort's location, in the heart of Punjab's Malwa region, was no accident. Bathinda lay on critical trade and invasion routes connecting Central Asia to Delhi and beyond. Its fort, over time, became a crucial stronghold for controlling northwest India.

Much of the structure as it appears today took shape in the 10th century under Raja Dab of the Hindu Shahi dynasty, and was later reinforced by the Ghaznavids, the Mughals, and even the Patiala princely state. Built of mud bricks and sandstone, the fort's most distinctive feature is its lofty rectangular structure with rounded bastions—rising nearly 36 meters high, visible from miles across the flat expanse of Punjab.

But Qila Mubarak is perhaps most famously linked to one remarkable figure: Razia Sultan, the first and only woman to sit on the throne of Delhi. It was here that she was imprisoned in 1240 after being overthrown, betrayed by the very nobles who once praised her. The lonely fort walls still seem to echo with her dignity, her rebellion, and her fall.

Though it has seen sieges and shifts in power—from the Mughals to the Marathas to the British—the fort was never entirely abandoned. It continued to be used as a garrison, a treasury, and now, a museum and monument. Recent conservation efforts have uncovered ancient coins, pottery, and even Roman relics—reminders of how deeply history runs beneath these stones.

Today, Qila Mubarak stands in the center of a bustling modern city, surrounded by traffic and towers. But it remains a vertical statement of resilience, whispering old stories above the new.

Gobindgarh Fort, Punjab

The Iron Heart of the Sikh Empire

(Sikh Empire under Maharaja Ranjit Singh, 18th–19th centuries)

Tucked in the vibrant center of Amritsar, not far from the sanctified serenity of the Golden Temple, lies a very different kind of monument: the Gobindgarh Fort.

Originally constructed by the Bhangi Misl in the 1760s, a confederation of Sikh warrior clans, the fort was significantly expanded and fortified under Maharaja Ranjit Singh, the Lion of Punjab. He named it after Guru Gobind Singh, the tenth Sikh Guru, and transformed it into the military nerve center of the Sikh Empire.

Designed with clear martial intention, Gobindgarh was an iron-clad fortress of strategy. It sprawled across 43 acres, surrounded by high walls and a deep moat. Four strong gates controlled access—most famously the Nalwa Gate, named after General Hari Singh Nalwa, one of Ranjit Singh's fiercest commanders. Inside the fort, arsenals, granaries, and barracks were constructed with industrial efficiency.

But it was not just a garrison. Gobindgarh also served as the treasury for Ranjit Singh's empire—and at its heart was said to rest the legendary Koh-i-Noor diamond, guarded within the Toshakhana (royal treasury) before it passed, through conquest and colonialism, into British hands.

Under British rule, the fort was adapted into a cantonment, stripped of its sovereign symbolism but never of its defiant spirit. Even in the 20th century, it remained an active military post under the Indian Army until its decommissioning.

Today, Gobindgarh Fort has been reborn as a heritage complex—but it wears its new identity with historical pride. Its restored ramparts host museums, cultural performances, exhibitions of Sikh martial arts (*Gatka*), and 7D shows recounting the life of Maharaja Ranjit Singh. Visitors walk its cobbled paths not as subjects, but as seekers—of knowledge, of pride, of continuity.

Gobindgarh stands as a reminder that fortresses were not always about land—they were about identity. It is where steel met spirit, and empire was measured not in territory, but in tenacity.

Ranthambhore Fort, Rajasthan

Immersed in the Stillness Where the Jungle Wears a Crown

(Chauhan Dynasty to Mughal Era, 10th–18th centuries)

Few forts in India possess the kind of mythic atmosphere that Ranthambhore does. It is not just the height of its ramparts or the depth of its moat—it is the fact that, centuries after its last battle, it remains alive. Alive with the breath of the jungle. Alive with the ghosts of kings, queens, and rebels. And alive with tigers.

Perched atop a 700-foot-high hill within what is today the Ranthambhore National Park, the fort dates back to the 10th century and was most famously ruled by the Chauhan dynasty. The name that resonates most within these ramparts is Hamir Dev Chauhan, a Rajput king who defied the Delhi Sultanate in the 13th century. His resistance to Alauddin Khilji became legendary—and his eventual defeat, tragic. Yet it was in Ranthambhore that Hamir created his last stand, and in doing so, he transformed the fort into a symbol of Rajput pride.

Ranthambhore's location made it a prize and a puzzle. Situated between north and central India, it guarded crucial trade routes while commanding panoramic views of the surrounding forested plains. Its walls, thick and winding, enclose temples, stepwells, palaces, and granaries. And unlike most hill forts, Ranthambhore's sheer elevation made it nearly impossible to siege without severe attrition.

After the Chauhans, the fort passed to various rulers—the Mughals used it more as a hunting lodge than a strategic outpost, a reflection of its transformation from frontier post to forested retreat. Today, Ranthambhore Fort lies within one of India's most famous tiger reserves, and visitors who climb its steep paths may be lucky enough to spot a striped monarch prowling below the battlements.

It is now a UNESCO World Heritage Site, not just for its architecture, but for its integration of culture, landscape, and history. Tigers walk where kings once did. Roots crack open ancient stone. And above it all, the Trinetra Ganesh Temple still draws thousands of devotees—proof that devotion, like wilderness, never dies.

Mehrangarh Fort, Rajasthan

The Citadel in the Clouds

(Period of Relevance: Rathore Dynasty (15th–20th centuries)

Rising 400 feet above the Blue City of Jodhpur, Mehrangarh's profile is unmistakable—walls that grow directly out of the cliff, as if the earth itself were waging its own war against time.

Founded in 1459 by Rao Jodha, the chief of the Rathore clan, who shifted his capital from the vulnerable Mandore plains to this rocky outcrop known as Bhakurcheeria, or the Mountain of Birds, legend has it that to build the fort, a hermit named Cheeria Nathji had to be displaced—he cursed the construction, claiming it would always suffer from drought. To appease the gods, Rao Jodha is said to have buried a man named Rajiya Bambi alive in the foundations, a chilling ritual of loyalty and sacrifice that still haunts Mehrangarh's origin story.

Mehrangarh sprawls across 1,200 acres and houses a series of palaces, courtyards, galleries, and temples. Its seven gates—each built to commemorate a victory—open into worlds within worlds. The Lohapol (Iron Gate), still bears the handprints of royal satis—queens who immolated themselves on their husband's funeral pyre. The Phool Mahal dazzles with gold filigree and stained glass; the Sheesh Mahal glitters with mirrorwork. And from every jharokha and parapet, the desert stretches endlessly into the horizon.

The Rathore rulers of Jodhpur were connoisseurs of art, music, and literature. Under Maharaja Jaswant Singh and later Maharaja Takht Singh, Mehrangarh became a center for Rajasthani painting, poetic patronage, and courtly refinement—even as it withstood battles against the Mughals and later, alliances with the British.

Mehrangarh has been preserved and revitalized by its custodians, particularly Gaj Singh II, the current Maharaja, who transformed the fort into one of India's finest cultural institutions. Today, the Mehrangarh Museum Trust curates exquisite collections of arms, costumes, miniature paintings, and palanquins. The fort also hosts festivals—like the Rajasthan International Folk Festival and World Sacred Spirit Festival—that echo with music instead of musket fire. From its highest points, the blue houses of Jodhpur shimmer below like a painted offering, and the wind, as it rushes through latticed windows, carries with it the soul of centuries.

Jaigarh Fort, Rajasthan

The Eye Above Amber

(Kachhwaha Rajput Rule, 17th–18th centuries)

If Amber was the palace, Jaigarh was the sword. Perched atop the Cheel Ka Teela—the Hill of Eagles—in the Aravalli range, Jaigarh Fort commands an unbroken view of Amber Fort below and the dry plains stretching toward Jaipur. Built in 1726 by Sawai Jai Singh II, the same ruler who would go on to build Jaipur itself, Jaigarh wasn't a royal residence or ceremonial showpiece. It was a fully functional military outpost, designed to protect Amber from siege and betrayal.

Everything about Jaigarh is martial. The walls stretch over 3 kilometers, wide enough for entire armies to march upon. Its towers and turrets are blunt, brutal, and effective. Hidden within the fort's thick walls were foundries, granaries, water tanks, and armories—the infrastructure of siege-resistance. The fort never fell. It was never even seriously attacked.

But what gives Jaigarh its enduring mystique is not just its strength—it is its secrets. For centuries, legend held that a vast royal treasure lay buried within its depths. In the 1970s, the Indian government, acting on rumors, conducted a search for gold and jewels, even deploying metal detectors and excavation teams. Nothing was found—but the story stuck.

And then there's the Jaivana Cannon, still mounted proudly on the ramparts. Cast in 1720 within the fort's own foundry, the Jaivana is one of the largest wheeled cannons ever made. Though it was only fired once—in a test—the legend goes that its shot flew nearly 35 kilometers.

Inside the fort, the architecture is sparse compared to Amber's opulence. The Vijay Garh Palace is modest. The Lakshmi Vilas and Aram Mandir are functional. But the real wonder of Jaigarh lies in its military design: covered passages, subterranean reservoirs, escape routes, and a meticulous water-harvesting system that allowed it to outlast long sieges. While Amber dreamed, Jaigarh watched.

Junagarh Fort, Rajasthan

The Desert Fortress That Never Fell

(Rathore Rule under Raja Rai Singh and Successors, 16th–20th centuries)

Most desert forts seek altitude. Junagarh chose audacity. Built not on a hilltop but on the open plains of Bikaner, Junagarh defied both geography and military convention.

Construction began in 1589 under Raja Rai Singh, a general in the Mughal emperor Akbar's court. With the wealth and favor he amassed in campaigns as far as Kabul and the Deccan, Rai Singh returned to Bikaner with the vision to build a fortress that matched his rising stature. By 1594, Junagarh was complete—a sprawling complex of bastions, courtyards, palaces, temples, and gardens encircled by a moat and high sandstone walls.

And remarkably, despite being exposed and accessible, the fort was never permanently conquered in battle—not even during the frequent skirmishes between Rajput states, or the Maratha intrusions of later centuries. It stood firm, shielded by its design and bolstered by its diplomacy.

But Junagarh was not just a fort—it was a stage for statecraft and ceremony. Its inner palaces are among the most exquisite in Rajasthan. The Anup Mahal gleams with gold-leaf walls and red glass inlay; the Phool Mahal breathes with floral elegance. The Chandra Mahal, with its delicate mirrorwork, and the Karan Mahal, with intricate lattice windows, speak of centuries where aesthetics and authority went hand in hand.

Junagarh also houses rare artefacts—ancient manuscripts, royal thrones, weapons, and the curious sight of a Second World War-era biplane gifted to the Maharaja by the British, now resting in the fort's museum.

Under British suzerainty, Bikaner remained one of the most loyal princely states, and Junagarh evolved with the times. Additions continued into the early 20th century, blending Mughal, Rajput, and European styles into a hybrid architecture that feels seamless. The fort was renamed Junagarh—'Old Fort'—after the royal family shifted their residence to the Lalgarh Palace nearby. But the old fort remains the true soul of Bikaner. Today, Junagarh is one of Rajasthan's best-preserved forts. The desert sun still burns down, but Junagarh, like the city it guards, does not wilt.

Taragarh Fort, Rajasthan

The Painted Fortress of Forgotten Kings

(Chauhan and Hada Rajput Dynasties, 14th–18th centuries)

You ascend into Taragarh Fort through a winding road that curls through Bundi's ancient lanes, past blue-washed houses, stepwells, and the slow life of a town untroubled by time. And then, suddenly, the climb begins—steep, stony, and flanked by jungles. At its summit, like a mirage made of battlements, waits Taragarh.

Also known as the Star Fort, Taragarh was constructed in the mid-14th century, though Bundi itself had been settled by the Chauhans even earlier. It was later developed into a royal stronghold by the Hada Rajputs, a branch of the Chauhan clan, who ruled Bundi with quiet dignity while mightier kingdoms battled over Rajasthan's deserts.

Unlike the massive stone blocks of Jodhpur or the precision symmetry of Jaipur, Taragarh is intimate, rambling, and half-swallowed by the mountain it crowns. Its walls are thick with moss and memory. Many parts have crumbled, yet what remains suggests a fort that once bloomed with grace: faded murals, whispering balconies, and a palace complex that housed some of the finest miniature paintings in India. The Chhatra Mahal, added by Rao Chattar Sal in the 17th century, is the artistic heart of the fort. Here, frescoes burst with color—depicting Krishna's lilas, royal processions, hunting scenes, and the rhythms of courtly life. Bundi's miniature painting school, nurtured within these walls, influenced all of Rajasthan's later artistic traditions. Yet Taragarh was not all art. It had teeth. Its fortifications included powerful bastions like the Bhim Burj, which once mounted a gargantuan cannon. Its three reservoirs—Rani Kund, Bhairav Kund, and Sukh Mahal Kund—harvested rainwater with ingenious efficiency, ensuring the fort could withstand siege for months.

But over time, Bundi's political relevance faded. Overshadowed by Jaipur and Kota, and later drawn into British dominion, the town and its fort slowly slipped into obscurity. Taragarh was never destroyed—but it was, quietly, abandoned.

Today, Taragarh Fort is both ruin and reverie. Langurs perch on parapets. Wind whistles through broken archways. Tourists arrive in ones and twos, always wide-eyed, always surprised that something so beautiful has been so forgotten.

Lohagarh Fort, Rajasthan

The Fort That Would Not Fall

(Jat Rule under Maharaja Suraj Mal and Successors, 18th–19th centuries)

Tucked away in Bharatpur, Lohagarh doesn't look like much at first—low, unadorned walls of earth and stone, far from the soaring battlements of Jaipur or the elegance of Udaipur. But Lohagarh's true strength was never in appearances. It was in resolve.

Built in the early 18th century by Maharaja Suraj Mal, the most formidable ruler of the Jat dynasty, Lohagarh was designed with one singular aim: to resist. And it did. Over and over again. The fort's name means 'Iron Fort,' and though it is made of mud mixed with bricks and lime, it lived up to that title. Its defenses were revolutionary for their time. Instead of tall walls prone to cannon damage, Lohagarh used massive earthen ramparts that absorbed artillery fire. It was surrounded by wide moats, with drawbridges and limited access points. The design was less about grandeur and more about calculated stubbornness. And stubborn it was.

When the British, under Lord Lake, laid siege to Lohagarh in 1805, they brought everything they had—cannons, infantry, even military engineering. But the fort refused to break. After months of bombardment, over a thousand British casualties, and still no breach, the invaders withdrew. Lohagarh had done what no other fort in Rajasthan had managed in that era—it had stood undefeated against the British Empire.

Inside the fort, the Jawahar Burj and Fateh Burj towers were built to commemorate victories against the Mughals and the British. These are not ornamental towers—they are statements, rendered in stone and grit. The inner quarters include palaces like the Kishori Mahal and Kothi Khas, which are modest compared to Rajput standards but functional and stately.

Lohagarh also housed administrative offices, armories, temples, and granaries. It was not a citadel of luxury, but a well-oiled machine of resistance. Even as Bharatpur's political fortunes shifted under colonial control, the memory of Lohagarh remained intact—as a place where Jat pride and military ingenuity held the line. Today, the fort is remarkably well preserved. It's a reminder that strength does not always wear splendor.

Sindhudurg Fort, Maharashtra

Shivaji Maharaj's Sea Bastion

(Maratha Empire under Chhatrapati Shivaji Maharaj, 17th–18th centuries)

In 1664, when the Western Ghats sloped into the Arabian Sea, and the Portuguese controlled most of the Konkan coast, Shivaji Maharaj knew that the sea had to become a shield. And so, he chose an island off the Malvan coast to build a fort like no other—one that would dominate the seaways, withstand foreign navies, and become the maritime heart of the Maratha Empire.

Construction of Sindhudurg began in 1664 and took three years. Over 100 Portuguese stone masons, 3,000 laborers, and nearly 500 *khandis* (tons) of iron were employed. The fort was built using molten lead to fuse the enormous laterite stone blocks—a technique that has allowed its massive walls to stand firm against not just time, but tide.

Spread across 48 acres, Sindhudurg's outer walls stretch nearly 3 kilometers, rising 30 feet high and 12 feet thick in places. It's not just a wall—it's a challenge to any ship that dared come close.

Yet for all its martial purpose, the fort is also a place of intimacy—because it is the only fort in India to house a temple dedicated to Shivaji Maharaj himself, built by his son Rajaram. The footprint of the great warrior-king, pressed into lime stone, is still preserved near the shrine.

The fort included 52 bastions, escape tunnels, freshwater wells (even on a salt-swept island), and barracks for over 2,000 soldiers. Cannons still point toward the horizon, their blackened mouths now filled with silence instead of fire.

Sindhudurg never fell to the Mughals or the Portuguese. Its only enemy, eventually, was time—and shifting tides of power. Under the British, the fort's naval significance diminished, though it was never abandoned. Today, it remains a site of pilgrimage, pride, and preservation.

To reach Sindhudurg, one must take a short ferry from Malvan. As the boat approaches, the fort appears suddenly—like a shadow rising from the water, edged in ramparts and memory. The sea laps at its stones, but it does not enter. Even today, the fortress holds the line.

Pratapgad Fort, Maharashtra

Where Strategy Met the Sword

(Maratha Empire under Shivaji Maharaj, 17th century)

Built in 1656 by Shivaji Maharaj, high above the coastal plains of Maharashtra, Pratapgad Fort was never intended as a city or ceremonial seat. It was a fort of intent—militarily precise, topographically brilliant, and destined to host one of Indian history's most pivotal personal encounters.

The location was chosen for its strategic vantage—overlooking the road to the coastal Konkan region. Shivaji needed a fort to consolidate his western dominion and to protect the recently conquered territories. But more urgently, it was here, in 1659, that a reckoning would take place between two men and two empires.

Afzal Khan, a general of the Adil Shahi Sultanate of Bijapur, was sent to crush Shivaji's rising rebellion. Known for his brute force and political cunning, Afzal Khan hoped to intimidate Shivaji into submission. But Shivaji was never one for the expected.

A peace meeting was arranged at Pratapgad, each leader to be accompanied by a small, unarmed escort. Shivaji, slight in stature and deeply aware of Afzal Khan's reputation, wore concealed armor and hid a weapon called the *wagh nakh*—steel claws—inside his glove. As the two embraced in the tent, Afzal Khan attempted to assassinate Shivaji with a hidden dagger. Shivaji struck first. Afzal Khan fell, and with him, the illusion that the Marathas could be subjugated easily.

That single moment—half myth, half meticulously plotted counterstrike—transformed Shivaji from local warlord to sovereign power. Pratapgad became sacred ground in the Maratha psyche.

The fort itself is divided into the upper and lower levels, with strong bastions, hidden stairways, and a commanding view of the valleys below. A temple to Bhavani Mata, Shivaji's patron goddess, stands within the fort—a quiet tribute to the spiritual force that shaped his military resolve. Nearby, a tall equestrian statue of Shivaji, sword aloft, overlooks the valley like a sentinel reborn. Unlike many forts that slowly decayed with time, Pratapgad has been preserved with care and reverence.

Ahmednagar Fort, Maharashtra

Where a Prison Became a Library

(Nizam Shahi Dynasty to British Raj, 15th–20th centuries)

Some forts are remembered for the wars they won. Ahmednagar Fort is remembered for the book it gave birth to behind bars. Built in the late 15th century by Malik Ahmad Nizam Shah I, founder of the Nizam Shahi dynasty, the fort was initially a stronghold of emerging Deccan power. Situated on the plains between Pune and Aurangabad, its location made it a coveted possession for every empire that ever tried to govern the Deccan—from the Mughals to the Marathas to the British.

It was under Akbar in the early 17th century that the fort was first annexed into the Mughal Empire, marking the slow decline of the Nizam Shahi rulers. Over time, it changed hands again, eventually coming under Scindia rule, and finally falling into British control in the 19th century.

Architecturally, Ahmednagar Fort is formidable. Shaped in a near-perfect circle and surrounded by a wide moat, its walls are thick and expansive. The fort's bastions rise at regular intervals, giving it the appearance of a disciplined military installation. Unlike the ornate palaces of Rajasthan or the dramatic cliffs of Maharashtra's hill forts, Ahmednagar is built for function over flair—its clean lines echoing its martial discipline.

But Ahmednagar's most lasting story is not one of dynastic intrigue, but of democratic resolve. In 1942, following the launch of the Quit India Movement, the British arrested key Congress leaders en masse. Pandit Jawaharlal Nehru, along with several other members of the Congress Working Committee, was imprisoned in Ahmednagar Fort for over a year. It was here, in that long enforced solitude, that Nehru wrote *The Discovery of India*—a sweeping narrative of Indian history, culture, and identity that would come to shape how independent India saw itself.

The fort, thus, became a paradox—built to restrain enemies, it gave birth to ideas that would eventually unshackle a nation. Today, Ahmednagar Fort is under the control of the Indian Army. Much of its structure remains intact, though access is limited. A few rooms, including Nehru's cell, have been preserved.

Vellore Fort, Tamil Nadu

The Granite Crossroads of Revolt and Faith

(Vijayanagara Empire to British Era, 16th–19th centuries)

There are few forts in India as perfectly preserved and yet as layered in complexity as Vellore Fort. Built in the 16th century by the powerful Vijayanagara rulers, the fort was a southern stronghold in the face of rising Deccan threats. But over time, Vellore would become a crucible of rebellion, a sanctuary of spirituality, and a silent witness to colonial confrontation.

Constructed almost entirely from massive granite blocks, Vellore Fort was engineered with exacting precision. Surrounded by a wide moat fed by subterranean springs and featuring double-layered ramparts, the fort was one of the most impenetrable in South India. It sprawled over a hundred acres and included bastions, parade grounds, granaries, palaces, and hidden tunnels. It was not just a defensive fortress—it was a self-contained city.

After the fall of the Vijayanagara Empire, the fort passed through several hands: the Bijapur Sultans, the Marathas, and then the Carnatic Nawabs, each of whom left behind their own architecture and influences. But its defining chapter came under the British East India Company. In 1806, long before 1857 made rebellion a national affair, Vellore Fort witnessed the first major military mutiny against British rule. Indian sepoys, angered by enforced changes in dress code that disrespected both Hindu and Muslim customs, rose up in the early hours of July 10. They stormed the fort, killed several British officers, and unfurled rebellion. Though the uprising was brutally suppressed, it sent shockwaves across the empire.

Within its walls stand three remarkable places of worship—side by side. The Jalakanteswarar Temple, an exquisite example of Dravidian stone carving with its towering gopuram; a mosque built during the Arcot Nawab's reign; and a modest but historic St. John's Church, one of the earliest Anglican churches in South India. Here, devotion wears many faces.

Today, the fort is maintained by the Archaeological Survey of India. Visitors can walk its wide pathways, peer down into the cool moat, marvel at the temple carvings, and stand where soldiers once mutinied—and where cultures once mingled.

Rock Fort, Tamil Nadu

Where Gods and Guns Shared Stone

(Pallava Period to Nayak Rule, 6th–18th centuries)

Towering 273 feet above the bustling city of Tiruchirappalli, the Rock Fort sits atop a monolithic rock formation believed to be older than the Himalayas. It isn't vast. It isn't sprawling. And yet, it commands. From its summit, the Cauvery river winds into the distance, temples dot the skyline, and the wind seems to carry fragments of chants, cannons, and conquests.

The early history of the rock is devotional. The Pallavas carved cave temples into its base as early as the 6th century CE. Later, during the Chola and Pandya periods, the site remained spiritually active but strategically dormant. It was under the Madurai Nayaks in the 17th century that the rock was transformed into a full-fledged fortress.

The Nayaks recognized its tactical brilliance. They fortified the upper reaches, added guard posts, storage rooms, and garrisons. But rather than displace the temples already carved into the rock, they built around them. Thus, Rock Fort became a place where faith and firepower coexisted.

Climbing the 400-odd stone-cut steps, visitors pass first the Thayumanavar Temple, where Shiva is worshipped as a mother who came down from the rock to assist a devotee in labor. Higher still, the Ucchi Pillayar Temple—dedicated to Lord Ganesha—sits like a crown on the hill. At the summit, the fort's remains—bastions, watch towers, and small gun positions—whisper of military watches long past.

In the 18th century, the British saw the fort's potential and seized it during their southern campaigns. It became a key site during the Carnatic Wars, where control over South India was bitterly contested by colonial powers. But even amidst cannons and colonialism, the temples remained undisturbed—continuing a rhythm of prayer uninterrupted by politics.

Today, Rock Fort is one of Tamil Nadu's most iconic landmarks. Devotees climb for blessings, and tourists ascend for the view. Historians linger at every level, piecing together the overlapping footprints of dynasties, saints, and soldiers.

Gulbarga Fort, Karnataka

The Dome of the Deccan

(Bahmani Sultanate, 14th–16th centuries)

In the mid-14th century, as the Delhi Sultanate struggled to hold its grip over the southern provinces, the Deccan began to assert its own story. At its heart stood Gulbarga, and within it, the fort that would birth a new dynasty: the Bahmani Sultanate.

Founded by Ala-ud-Din Bahman Shah in 1347 after a successful rebellion against the Delhi Sultanate's weakening hold, Gulbarga Fort was expanded from an earlier Hindu stronghold into a formidable capital—part citadel, part cultural manifesto. It became the first official seat of the Bahmani kingdom, before the capital later shifted to Bidar.

The fort sprawls over 38,000 square meters and is enclosed by a double line of fortifications, punctuated by 15 towers and surrounded by a wide moat—filled then, as now, by monsoon-fed water. The military architecture was solid, but what sets Gulbarga apart is the ethereal beauty at its center: the Jama Masjid, one of India's oldest and most unique mosques.

Unlike the open courtyards of typical South Asian mosque architecture, the Jama Masjid at Gulbarga is entirely enclosed—its roof supported by 250 arches and domes, creating a prayer hall that feels like a forest of stone. Built in 1367 and inspired by Spain's Great Mosque of Córdoba, it is a masterpiece of Indo-Islamic architecture, imbued with Persian and Central Asian influences.

The mosque was never part of a city—it was part of the fort itself, a rare and deliberate gesture of merging military strength with spiritual identity. And that, perhaps, is the lasting metaphor of Gulbarga: it was not just a power center but a melting pot, where soldiers, scholars, mystics, and artisans carved a Deccan distinct from both north and south.

Though the Bahmani capital eventually shifted and fragmented into the five Deccan Sultanates, Gulbarga remained a cultural touchstone—later ruled by the Adil Shahis of Bijapur and then absorbed into the Nizam's Hyderabad State under the Asaf Jahis. Today, Gulbarga's fort walls still stand, encasing the Jama Masjid like a memory sealed in time. The site is serene, with the echoes of centuries of prayer, scholarship, and diplomacy.

Bijapur Fort, Karnataka

Where the Sultan's Whisper Lingers

(Adil Shahi Dynasty, 15th–17th centuries)

If Gulbarga laid the foundation of the Deccan Sultanates, Bijapur perfected their grandeur. Founded by Yusuf Adil Shah after the splintering of the Bahmani Empire, the Adil Shahis made Bijapur their capital, and for nearly two centuries, they poured their might, taste, and ambition into its stone. The result: a fortified city where every arch led to acoustics, and every dome dared gravity.

Bijapur Fort, more a walled city than a singular citadel, encompassed palaces, mosques, gardens, barracks, and bastions—sprawling over 10 square kilometers. It was less about vertical might and more about spatial mastery. Wide avenues led to inner citadels, and massive gates like the Makka Gate and Shivgiri Gate announced the city's plural identity—equal parts Persianate refinement and South Indian grounding.

Above all, Bijapur is synonymous with one structure: the Gol Gumbaz. Commissioned by Muhammad Adil Shah in the 17th century as his mausoleum, the Gol Gumbaz 'Round Dome'—is the second-largest free-standing dome in the world after St. Peter's Basilica in Rome. It is neither supported by columns nor restrained by buttresses. Instead, it rests on thick walls and a confidence in Deccan engineering. Stand at the center of the inner chamber and speak a word—it will echo seven times. Even whispers, they say, travel across the chamber with perfect clarity.

Yet Gol Gumbaz is no outlier. The Ibrahim Rauza, tomb of Ibrahim Adil Shah II, is considered a forerunner to the Taj Mahal in form and grace. The Jama Masjid, begun by Ali Adil Shah I, is monumental, its prayer hall supported by majestic arches.

The fort complex also contains waterworks, pleasure pavilions, armories, and audience halls. Under the Adil Shahis, Bijapur became a center of learning, music, and Sufi philosophy. In 1686, Aurangzeb's Mughal army marched south and annexed Bijapur, ending the Adil Shahi dynasty. Today, the fort's many monuments remain scattered across the city, some in active use, others in gentle ruin.

Srirangapatna Fort, Karnataka

The Island That Roared

(Wodeyar Dynasty to Tipu Sultan, 17th–18th centuries)

To reach Srirangapatna, one crosses a narrow bridge over the Cauvery. The fort at the heart of the island town is modest in size, but it was here that Tipu Sultan made his last stand against the British, where a vision of a sovereign Mysore breathed its final defiant breath.

First fortified by the Wodeyar rulers in the 17th century, the original mud fort was later expanded and strengthened in stone by Hyder Ali and his son Tipu Sultan in the 18th century. With thick walls, ramparts built in European style, and gateways on all four cardinal directions, Srirangapatna was a hybrid of eastern purpose and western strategy.

At its peak, the fort was a full royal capital. Inside lay palaces, temples, a mosque, a mint, and an arsenal. The most celebrated structure was the Daria Daulat Bagh, Tipu's summer palace, made not of stone but of teak, its walls and ceilings adorned with vibrant murals depicting scenes of diplomacy, war, and celebration. One wall shows the Battle of Pollilur—Tipu's greatest victory over the British—where rockets streak through the sky and East India Company troops fall in disarray.

Tipu Sultan, an innovator as well as a warrior, famously developed Mysorean rockets, one of the earliest metal-cylinder rocket systems ever used in warfare. These were launched from Srirangapatna. But in 1799, during the Fourth Anglo-Mysore War, British forces breached the fort. Tipu was killed in battle near the Water Gate, defending his city to the very end.

Today, the fort's walls still stand, enclosing a town that is part pilgrimage, part battlefield, part museum. The Gumbaz, Tipu's mausoleum, lies just outside the fort—white domed, silent, and surrounded by his family's tombs. The Jama Masjid within the fort still hosts prayers, and the Sri Ranganathaswamy Temple, from which the town takes its name, predates even the fort itself. It is a place where you feel the push and pull of time—of what was gained, lost, and still fiercely remembered.

Orchha Fort Complex, Madhya Pradesh

A Kingdom Caught in Reverie

(Bundela Dynasty, 16th–18th centuries)

Tucked away on a seasonal island in the Betwa River, Orchha is a place where history never quite hardened into ruin. Founded in 1531 by Rudra Pratap Singh, the fort complex served as the capital of the Bundela Rajputs, a fiercely independent clan.

Orchha's palaces are not arranged in strict military symmetry but in lyrical tiers, domes floating above arcaded courtyards, bridges curving across water, and temples that rise like meditations in stone. At its heart stands the Raja Mahal, built by Madhukar Shah. From the outside, it is severe—thick walls, limited ornamentation. But inside, it blooms. The walls and ceilings are covered in exquisite frescoes—depicting scenes from the Ramayana, celestial beings, and devotional iconography in a fusion of Mughal and Rajput styles.

Next to it, the Jahangir Mahal—built by Bir Singh Deo to welcome the Mughal emperor Jahangir—is a triumph of Rajput-Mughal architecture. Its symmetrical balconies, delicate latticework, and soaring domes are all designed to impress. Legend has it that Jahangir stayed only for one night, but the building remains his grandest suite in absentia.

The complex also includes the Sheesh Mahal (now a heritage hotel), watchtowers, courtyards, and temples—including the towering Chaturbhuj Temple, whose spire dominates the skyline, and the Ram Raja Temple, where Lord Ram is worshipped not as a deity but as a king, with sentries and guards in full regalia.

What makes Orchha hauntingly beautiful is its setting. The Betwa flows gently beside it, mirroring domes in its waters. The surrounding forest and farmland encase the complex like a forgotten tale. Orchha was never a dominant kingdom in political terms, but it understood pageantry. Today, the fort complex is a quiet jewel—often bypassed by tourists rushing toward Khajuraho or Gwalior. But for those who stay, Orchha offers one of the most romantic and reflective experiences of any Indian fort. Here, you don't just see history—you feel it thinking.

Mandu Fort, Madhya Pradesh

The Kingdom of Love and Stone

(Paramara to Malwa Sultanate, 10th–16th centuries)

Built atop the rugged Vindhya hills, the Mandu Fort complex spreads over 80 square kilometers, one of the largest fortified zones in India. It first rose under the Paramara rulers in the 10th century but came into its full flowering under the Sultans of Malwa, especially Ghiyas-ud-din Khalji, whose court became a swirl of Persian refinement and local aesthetic.

Yet for all its military architecture—thick ramparts, multiple gates, water tanks, and defensive outposts—Mandu's soul is not in its war rooms. It lies in the sigh between two names: Baz Bahadur and Rani Roopmati.

Baz Bahadur, the last independent Sultan of Malwa, was a warrior-poet who fell in love with Roopmati, a Hindu singer of sublime talent. Their romance is said to have filled the halls of Mandu with music and moonlight. The Rewa Kund, a reservoir built for Roopmati to perform her daily worship of the Narmada River, and the Roopmati Pavilion, perched on the edge of the plateau, bear silent witness to this bond. The love story ended tragically—Akbar's army marched in, Baz Bahadur fled, and Roopmati, refusing to be captured, took her own life. But Mandu never let go of their names.

Elsewhere within the complex rises the Jahaz Mahal, or 'Ship Palace,' so called because during the monsoon it seems to float between two artificial lakes. This 15th-century pleasure palace, with its long colonnades and rooftop pavilions, captures the leisure-loving spirit of Ghiyas-ud-din Khalji, who housed hundreds of women in his court and created for them a world of music, gardens, and courtyards.

There is also the Hindola Mahal, or 'Swing Palace,' its slanted buttresses giving the illusion of motion, the Jami Masjid, inspired by Damascus's great mosque, and Hoshang Shah's Tomb, India's first marble mausoleum—an architectural prototype for the Taj Mahal.

Over centuries, Mandu was besieged, conquered, and eventually abandoned, but its ruins remain curiously alive. Bougainvillea spills over broken arches. Today, Mandu is visited less for its strategic brilliance and more for the haunting beauty of its collapse.

Rohtasgarh Fort, Bihar

The Bastion of Betrayal and Ascent

(Sher Shah Suri to Mughal Rule, 16th–18th centuries)

You arrive at Rohtasgarh through thick forest, over narrow trails, and past the hush of birds. Perched 1,500 feet above sea level on the Rohtas plateau, the fort is vast—over 4,000 acres—and nearly invisible until you're right at its feet. Its isolation is its strategy, and its story is one of treachery, strategy, and remarkable survival.

Though the origins of the fort predate recorded history—it is mentioned in ancient Jain and Hindu texts—the structure that looms today owes much to the 16th century and the ambitions of Sher Shah Suri, the Afghan ruler who briefly snatched the Mughal throne from Humayun and built a parallel imperial structure of astonishing efficiency.

Sher Shah is said to have seized Rohtas through cunning: he requested permission from the Hindu raja to station his womenfolk in the fort for protection. Once granted, his soldiers—disguised as women—entered and captured it from within. From this act of deception, Sher Shah gained control of one of the strongest forts in eastern India.

Rohtas became a key outpost in his empire, overseeing the route between the Gangetic plains and central India. Its design is immense: multiple gates (the Hathiya Pol, or Elephant Gate, is the grandest), hundreds of wells and tanks, palaces like the Baradari, audience halls, secret escape routes, and barracks spread across a rugged hillscape.

After Sher Shah's death, the Mughals took control, and the fort became a garrison and prison. It was later occupied by rebellious zamindars, passed to the British during the colonial period, and eventually slipped into decay. But its defenses—massive stone walls, deep ditches, and narrow access routes—remained largely untouched.

Even today, Rohtasgarh is not easily accessible. There's no road to the top. The climb takes hours. But those who reach it are rewarded with something few Indian forts offer: solitude that feels holy, and views that stretch beyond centuries.

Barabati Fort, Odisha

The Citadel on the Mahanadi

(Eastern Ganga to Mughal-British Era, 11th–18th centuries)

At the northern edge of Cuttack, where the Mahanadi River once flowed in fuller song, the ruins of Barabati Fort sit quietly—its moat overgrown, its gateways sunlit and silent. But this was once the strategic and symbolic heart of Odisha, guarding a capital whose name—Kataka—literally meant 'military encampment.' In its heyday, Barabati wasn't just a fort. It was a fulcrum.

The fort's foundations were laid in the 11th century, during the reign of the Eastern Ganga dynasty, a line of kings more famously associated with temple grandeur, such as the Sun Temple at Konark. But it was under the Gajapati kings in the 14th and 15th centuries that Barabati became a full-fledged military and administrative stronghold. Its location at the delta of the Mahanadi made it a vital point for inland river trade and coastal defense—open to opportunity but also vulnerable to invasion.

The fort was originally built of laterite and sandstone, laid out in a nearly square plan, with a wide moat fed by the river, and fortified gateways at its east and west. Inside, it housed palaces, arsenals, temples, and a durbar hall—of which only scant ruins remain today. Its strategic design reflected not just defense but ceremony, built to host kings and withstand storms.

Over time, as power shifted eastward and invaders descended from Bengal and the north, Barabati Fort became a prized possession. The Afghans of Bengal, the Mughals, and eventually the Marathas each left their mark on its walls, using it as a military outpost and administrative center.

In the 18th century, the British took over the fort, transforming parts of it into a residence and later, a jail. Like many colonial occupations, they left the structure standing but sapped it of its ceremonial soul. Earthquakes and floods took care of the rest.

Today, only parts of the fort's ramparts, moat, and the 10th-century Ganga-era gate remain, holding the story of a coastal kingdom that once held its head high against the tide of empires.

Warangal Fort, Telangana

Where the Stones Spoke the Language of an Empire

(Kakatiya Dynasty, 12th–14th centuries)

In the 13th century, when northern India trembled under Mongol threats and Delhi reeled from internal strife, the southern Deccan bore witness to a different kind of empire—quietly confident, gracefully built. Warangal, under the Kakatiyas, emerged not through conquest, but through the cultural magnetism of art, administration, and architecture. And at its center stood Warangal Fort.

Founded by Rudra Deva and later fortified by Ganapati Deva and Rani Rudrama Devi, the fort was as much a capital as it was a declaration—that the Telugu-speaking heartland had its own vision of empire. Warangal Fort was designed in concentric circles: a mud inner fort, a stone-built outer fort, and finally, a massive stone wall with 45 towers and gateways surrounding the capital.

But what takes the breath away even today are the Kirti Toranas—four massive stone gateways carved from single rock formations, each over 30 feet high, still standing despite centuries of siege and ruin. They are not just gateways; they are sculptures of statehood, inscribed with floral motifs and mythical beasts, blending warfare with worship.

The city was a center of temple architecture and the literary arts. Rani Rudrama Devi, one of the few reigning queens in Indian history, ruled from here with wisdom and valor, continuing the expansion of irrigation systems, patronage of the arts, and military fortification. Later, Prataparudra, her grandson, would be the last great Kakatiya ruler—facing the might of the Delhi Sultanate as it swept south.

In 1323, Ulugh Khan—later Muhammad bin Tughlaq—stormed Warangal with massive forces. Though Prataparudra resisted valiantly, betrayal and overwhelming numbers led to the city's capture. The fort was plundered, and its decline began. Yet the Kakatiya spirit—grounded in regional pride and architectural brilliance—never vanished.

Today, the Kirti Toranas remain Warangal's emblem, even featured on the seal of the Government of Telangana. The fort area, though largely in ruins, still holds temple remains, water tanks, and scattered bastions.

Fort Aguada, Goa

Where an Empire Watched the Waves

(Portuguese Colonial Era, 17th–19th centuries)

To stand atop Fort Aguada, with wind in your hair and sea in your eyes, is to understand why the Portuguese came—and why they stayed. Built in 1612 to guard against Dutch and Maratha incursions, the fort wasn't just a bulwark of defense. It was a declaration of control over the sea, the spice route, and the shifting tides of colonial power.

The name Aguada means 'watering place' in Portuguese, and it refers to the freshwater springs near the site that once refreshed ships on long voyages. But what rose above those springs was a fortress of purpose. With 13-meter-high walls and a deep moat, the fort protected the vital port of Old Goa, at the time a glittering hub of Lusitanian commerce and faith in Asia.

Strategically located at the mouth of the Mandovi River, Fort Aguada could fire upon any incoming vessel long before it reached inland harbors. The architecture was Iberian in inspiration but adapted to Indian monsoon and terrain—angular bastions, dry laterite stone, and functional corridors designed to survive both cannon fire and tropical squalls.

Inside the fort's sprawling grounds was once housed a garrison, an ammunition room, and a massive cistern capable of storing 2.3 million gallons of water—enough to last a hundred men through a long siege. But the fort's most iconic feature remains the Aguada Lighthouse, built in 1864, the oldest of its kind in Asia, whose beacon lit the sea route to Goa for over a century.

The fort was never taken by force. It served more as a visual deterrent and a symbol of Portuguese authority. Later, it was used as a prison—a role it retained into post-Independence India. Some of its quarters were known for housing political prisoners during the colonial struggle.

Today, Fort Aguada is a major tourist destination—not just for its views over the Arabian Sea, but for what it represents: the intersection of exploration and occupation, ambition and architecture. The ramparts are peaceful now, and the sea still shimmers below—endlessly, watchfully.

St. Angelo Fort, Kerala

The Fort of Three Flags

(Portuguese, Dutch, and British Colonial Periods, 1505–20th centuries)

It began, as many colonial stories do, with a cross and a cannon. In 1505, Dom Francisco de Almeida, the first Portuguese Viceroy of India, built a triangular bastion on the edge of the sea at Kannur, then a strategic port ruled by the Kolathiri Rajas. Named St. Angelo Fort, it was among the earliest Portuguese forts in India, meant to secure spice trade routes and dominate the Malabar coast.

The fort's early history was one of splendor and betrayal. In 1509, de Almeida's own son, Lourenço, died in battle off Diu, and soon after, the Viceroy himself defied royal orders to return home, choosing instead to bury his grief and dig deeper into his coastal empire. The fort became a symbol of personal loyalty, Portuguese ambition—and eventually, vulnerability.

In 1663, the Dutch East India Company captured the fort and made extensive modifications, building bastions named Hollandia, Zeelandia, and Frieslandia, creating a low-lying structure with thick laterite walls and large ramparts that could withstand sea attacks. Under the Dutch, the fort also became a base for pepper trade and diplomacy with local rulers.

Later, the British took control in 1790 and garrisoned troops here for over a century, incorporating it into their chain of coastal control points. Each empire left its imprint in stone: Portuguese churches, Dutch warehouses, British barracks. Yet the architecture retained a singular function—defense by design, against both sea and ambition.

St. Angelo's position, jutting into the sea, offers sweeping views of the Dharmadom Island and the Moppila Bay, once teeming with trading vessels from Arabia, Africa, and Europe. The fort also houses an old chapel, a secret tunnel believed to lead to the sea, and several rusted cannons pointed forever at the horizon.

Today, it is a quiet sentinel, managed by the Archaeological Survey of India. The ramparts are free to walk, and schoolchildren lean on the walls where Dutch soldiers once crouched with muskets.

Palakkad Fort, Kerala

The Gateway Between Kingdoms

(Mysore Kingdom under Hyder Ali and Tipu Sultan, 18th century)

In the 18th century, when the British and Mysoreans battled not just for land, but for strategic access, the Palakkad Gap was a key prize. This 30-kilometer-wide opening in the Western Ghats was the easiest route from the east into Kerala's spice-rich Malabar coast. Whoever held the Palakkad Fort controlled the corridor. And Hyder Ali, the Sultan of Mysore, understood that perfectly.

Though the site had earlier fortifications attributed to the local Palakkad rajas, it was Hyder Ali who rebuilt and reinforced it in 1766, transforming it into a formidable garrison. The new design was compact but commanding—a square layout of granite walls, four corner bastions, and a broad moat. It didn't aim to impress; it aimed to endure.

The fort's main function was logistical. It allowed Mysorean forces, under Hyder and later Tipu Sultan, to launch quick campaigns across the Ghats and retreat as needed. Its location at the meeting point of highland and lowland gave it unmatched visibility and control. It became a military outpost, a supply base, and a thorn in the side of the East India Company.

In 1768, the British under Colonel Wood captured it, only to lose it again to Tipu. This game of tug-of-war continued through the Anglo-Mysore Wars until 1790, when the British finally took permanent control.

Under British rule, Palakkad Fort became an administrative center and prison. It saw no grand sieges or royal pageantry, but its strategic importance was always understood. Even today, standing within its thick stone walls, one senses its calculated simplicity—nothing wasted, everything watching.

The fort encloses a well-preserved inner courtyard, granaries, and a small temple. A later addition, the Middelburg Bastion, offers sweeping views of the town and surrounding countryside. The outer moat, once teeming with crocodiles and rain-fed water, is now crossed by footbridges and shaded by banyan trees. Today, Palakkad Fort is among the best-preserved forts in Kerala. Locals refer to it simply as the Tipu Sultan Fort, though Tipu himself only briefly held it.

Tughlaqabad Fort, Delhi

The City That Defied and Fell

(Delhi Sultanate under Ghiyas-ud-din Tughlaq, 14th century)

In the early 14th century, as Delhi bristled with rebellions and Mongol threats, Ghiyas-ud-din Tughlaq ascended the throne of the Delhi Sultanate with two things in mind: power and permanence. In 1321, he began building Tughlaqabad—a fort so vast it was meant to house not just an army, but an entire city. It would be Delhi's third city, its mightiest fortress, and the seat of a new dynasty's unshakable will. He finished it in four years.

The scale is staggering even today. Perched on a rocky outcrop of the Aravalli hills, the fort's massive sloping walls, some 10 to 15 meters high and up to 10 meters thick at the base, stretch across more than 6 square kilometers. Interspersed with 52 gates and bastions, its formidable profile seems less built than hewn—like it erupted from the earth. Ghiyas-ud-din wanted not delicacy, but dread. Yet the story of Tughlaqabad is as much about its fall as its rise.

According to legend, the great Sufi saint Nizamuddin Auliya, whose followers were building a *baoli* (stepwell) at the same time, cursed the fort when Ghiyas-ud-din tried to divert laborers for royal use. His words became prophecy: *'Ya rahe ujjar, ya base Gujjar'*—'either it will lie desolate, or be occupied by shepherds.' And so it did. The city, barely populated, fell into ruin not long after the sultan's sudden death—possibly orchestrated by his own son, Muhammad bin Tughlaq, a ruler more famed for eccentricity than consolidation.

Tughlaqabad's abandonment was accelerated by its poor water supply and its location—too exposed, too hard to sustain. But even in its ruin, it remained formidable. The inner citadel, with its royal quarters and granaries, the secret escape tunnels, and the outer bastions still offer a labyrinth of stone and silence.

Nearby, the austere yet majestic Tomb of Ghiyas-ud-din Tughlaq, built by the sultan himself, survives with red sandstone sloping walls and a white dome—a stark contrast to the ornate Mughal tombs that came later. Its pointed arches seem to gaze sternly at the city that never was.

Neemrana Fort Palace, Rajasthan

The Ruin That Rewrote Its Fate

(Chauhan Dynasty to Modern Heritage Revival, 15th century–present)

Perched on a rocky slope midway between Delhi and Jaipur, Neemrana Fort Palace was once just another forgotten sentinel of Rajputana—a structure with a name but no pulse. Built in 1464 by Raja Prithvi Raj Chauhan III's descendants, the fort served as the seat of the Chauhans of Neemrana, a small principality on the fringes of major power centers. For centuries, it witnessed the quiet churn of princely politics without ever becoming the stage for great conquests or catastrophe.

Then, it faded. By the mid-20th century, Neemrana lay in ruins. Its stone walls, once echoing with courtly deliberations and folk music, were silent. Trees grew through its courtyards. Bats roosted in its turrets. It became just another ghost in Rajasthan's gallery of abandoned splendors.

But unlike many of its peers, Neemrana was not left to crumble. In 1986, the property was acquired by Aman Nath and Francis Wacziarg, visionaries who believed that India's heritage could live again—not in museums, but in memories and experiences. Over years of painstaking restoration, the fort was transformed into India's first heritage hotel—not a replica of the past, but a living, breathing reinvention of it.

What emerged is a structure that has retained its medieval bones but moved to a modern rhythm. Terraced across twelve levels into the hillside, Neemrana Fort Palace now hosts rooms, courtyards, amphitheaters, hanging gardens, swimming pools, and even a zipline. Each room is named—not numbered—and furnished with a blend of antique and contemporary aesthetics, designed to immerse, not simply impress.

Visitors walk along ancient corridors, dine beneath Mughal arches, and sleep where rulers once plotted allegiances. No two spaces are alike; no two views the same. And always, beneath the luxury, lies stone worn smooth by centuries of sun, monsoon, and memory.

Neemrana has become a model for heritage conservation in India. It has proved that preservation need not be passive. It can be active, adaptive, and deeply alive. Other forts and palaces across India have followed its lead, but Neemrana remains the pioneer—the ruin that refused to die quietly.

Pavagadh Fort, Gujarat

The Sacred Hill That Withstood Time

(Chaulukya, Khichi Chauhan, and Gujarat Sultanate, 10th–16th centuries)

To climb Pavagadh is to ascend through myth and memory, passing Jain temples, ancient gates, ruined bastions, and finally, at the summit, a shrine to Kalikamata that draws pilgrims year-round. But beneath this sacred pilgrimage lies the skeleton of a fortress that once stood guard over Gujarat's destiny.

The earliest settlements on Pavagadh date back to the Chaulukya dynasty, whose rule in the 10th and 11th centuries seeded the first religious structures on the hill. But it was under the Khichi Chauhan Rajputs, and Mahmud Begada, that Pavagadh became a citadel of resistance and, eventually, conquest.

By the 14th century, the fort atop the hill became the capital of Champaner, a city at the base that would flourish briefly as one of Gujarat's grandest capitals. The fort walls stretched across miles of hillside terrain, fortified with a series of gates, bastions, and watchtowers that used the natural slope for strategic advantage. The Makai Gate, Budhiya Gate, and Atak Gate are just a few among the network that once controlled movement up the mountain.

In 1484, Sultan Mahmud Begada of the Gujarat Sultanate conquered Pavagadh after a prolonged siege, and what followed was remarkable: the birth of Champaner-Pavagadh as a combined urban-religious-military complex, eventually designated as a UNESCO World Heritage Site. Begada didn't destroy the sacred structures—he built around them. Champaner, at the foot of the hill, became a planned city with mosques, palaces, stepwells, and civic architecture, while the summit retained its Hindu spiritual significance.

Even in its prime, Pavagadh was more than a fortress—it was a vertical metaphor. From Jain temples partway up the hill to the Kalikamata Temple at the top, and the Islamic domes of Jami Masjid down below, it became a monument to Gujarat's layered religious and political history.

Today, most visitors come for the temple, reaching the summit by foot or ropeway, unaware that they are walking through one of India's most dramatic fortified complexes. The walls are weathered. Many bastions are broken. But the hill holds, as always.

Allahabad Fort, Uttar Pradesh

Where Empire Claimed the Confluence

(Mughal Empire, 16th–18th centuries, British Raj)

In 1583, the Mughal emperor Akbar stood at the Triveni Sangam—a place where the devout believed three rivers met, and time became eternal. And yet Akbar, ever the master of synthesis, did something extraordinary. He didn't just kneel at the river. He built above it. The result was Allahabad Fort—the largest Mughal fort in India, a monument to control, envision, and affect a spiritual-political fusion.

Constructed with red sandstone and local materials, the fort was designed to dominate both the sacred geography and the flow of goods and people through the Gangetic plain. Its walls stretch over 2 kilometers, enclosing a complex that once included royal quarters, gardens, bastions, and ceremonial halls.

The architecture, though largely militaristic, bore the finesse of Mughal symmetry and design. Massive gates, tall walls, and circular bastions were complemented by interior halls decorated with arches and *jali* windows. At the heart of the complex was the Zenana, or women's quarters, and a grand audience hall, all strategically placed to oversee both the river and the city.

But perhaps the most mysterious relic inside the fort is far older than Akbar himself—the Ashokan Pillar, a 35-foot-high sandstone monolith inscribed with the edicts of Emperor Ashoka from the 3rd century BCE. Akbar had it moved here from Kaushambi, embedding the Mauryan past into his own imperial present. The pillar is said to also carry later inscriptions by Samudragupta and Jahangir, making it a rare palimpsest of dynasties.

The fort also houses the Patalpuri Temple and the legendary Akshayavat, or 'immortal banyan tree,' said to be indestructible and revered by pilgrims for millennia. Akbar ensured that Hindu and local traditions were not erased but encased—part of his broader policy of inclusion through architecture.

In colonial times, the British took over the fort, converting much of it into a garrison and arsenal. They restricted access, built barracks, and dug into its stones with their own designs. Even today, large parts of the fort remain under the control of the Indian Army and are closed to the public.

Kangla Fort, Manipur

The Sacred Seat of the Sangai Kingdom

(Meitei Kingdom, 1st century CE–1891)

To walk through Kangla is to walk through Manipur's soul. More than just a fort, Kangla—which means 'dry land' in Meitei—was the political, religious, and cultural epicenter of the ancient Meitei Kingdom for almost two millennia. It was not raised suddenly by kings seeking conquest, but evolved organically through dynasties, belief systems, and rituals.

The origins of Kangla go back to Nongda Lairen Pakhangba, who ascended the throne in 33 CE and is considered the first historical ruler of Manipur. Over centuries, the site grew into a fortified capital—encircled by moats, gates, and sacred groves. It became the ceremonial seat of Meitei royalty, where coronations were conducted, rites performed, and sovereignty sanctified by the gods.

At its core stood the Kangla Uttra, the coronation hall; nearby, the Govindajee Temple and Kangla Sha—twin statues of the mythological dragon-lion guardian spirits that once flanked the fort's gates. These were not mere decorative creatures, but protectors of the land and its balance, symbolizing the fort's spiritual charge.

But Kangla was not untouched by violence. In 1891, after the Anglo-Manipur War, British troops stormed Kangla, defeated the Manipuri resistance, and took control of the complex. They razed the Kangla Sha, destroyed several shrines and buildings, and raised the Union Jack where the flag of Manipur once fluttered.

The fall of Kangla marked the end of Manipur's political independence. It became a princely state under British suzerainty, and the fort—long sacred and sovereign—was converted into a cantonment. The cultural rupture was profound, remembered today with both sorrow and resolve.

It was only in 2004, more than a century later, that Kangla was finally handed back to the people of Manipur by the Indian Army. Since then, it has been lovingly restored as a heritage site, spiritual nucleus, and symbol of Manipuri identity. The twin Kangla Sha have been resurrected. Ceremonies are again held within its precincts, and the past feels present—not in ruins, but in reverence.

Hampi (Vijayanagara Fort), Karnataka

The City That Dared to Dazzle

(Vijayanagara Empire, 14th–16th centuries)

There was a time when foreign travelers arrived at Hampi, stood atop the surrounding hills, and could not believe what they saw: bazaars that stretched for miles, gem merchants trading in the open, water channels engineered with surgical precision, and temples that rivalled palaces. 'This is no ordinary city,' wrote Domingo Paes, a 16th-century Portuguese chronicler, 'It is as large as Rome, and very beautiful to the sight.'

Hampi, the capital of the Vijayanagara Empire, was established in 1336 by Harihara I and Bukka Raya, and it quickly became the largest and most prosperous city in India—possibly the second-largest in the world at its peak. It was as much a spiritual center as it was a military marvel.

The fortifications of Hampi are extraordinary in concept and execution. Rather than walling in a single citadel, the empire turned the surrounding hills, boulders, and rivers into an organic defense system. Enormous granite enclosures followed the natural contours of the land. Defensive walls were not simply barriers—they were sculpted into the terrain.

At the center of this was the Royal Enclosure, a fortified campus of palaces, audience halls, underground chambers, and watchtowers. The Mahanavami Dibba, a grand platform used by kings during festivals and royal assemblies, still rises above the plains, engraved with scenes of processions and courtly life. Nearby stands the Queen's Bath, a blend of Indo-Islamic architecture, and the Hazara Rama Temple, whose friezes narrate the entire Ramayana in stone.

Hampi was sacred too. The Virupaksha Temple, dedicated to Lord Shiva, still functions as a place of worship today, as does the Vittala Temple, with its iconic stone chariot and musical pillars. In 1565, the combined armies of the Deccan Sultanates defeated the Vijayanagara forces at the Battle of Talikota. The victors plundered Hampi for six months. Temples were desecrated. Palaces were burned. Markets were flattened. And the empire vanished almost overnight. Yet the bones of Hampi remain. Scattered across 26 square kilometers, its ruins rise out of the earth like the embers of a vanished fire, now protected as a UNESCO World Heritage Site.

Fort Dansborg, Tamil Nadu

Where the Danes Met the Deccan

(Danish Colonial Period, 1620–1845)

It begins with a treaty. In 1620, Raghunatha Nayak, ruler of Tanjore, agreed to let the Danes establish a port and trading post at Tranquebar, a sleepy village hugged by the sea. In return, they would supply arms and ships to the Nayak's coastal campaigns. And so, under the command of Admiral Ove Gjedde, the Danish East India Company laid the foundation of Fort Dansborg, a long, low-slung bastion with thick ochre walls, white arches, and tiled roofs more familiar in Copenhagen than Chennai.

But it worked.

The fort was designed less for military defense and more as a fortified factory, governor's residence, and storehouse for spices, textiles, and pearls. Yet its form followed function elegantly. Facing the Bay of Bengal, its rooms were airy, with high ceilings and large windows—perfectly adapted to tropical heat. A chapel and a bell tower followed soon after, and Fort Dansborg became not only the headquarters of Danish trade but also of Danish Christianity in India.

The Danes were never major players in Indian colonization. But from Fort Dansborg, they quietly conducted a brisk business in pepper, cloth, and missionaries. One of the most significant legacies of their presence is the arrival of Bartholomäus Ziegenbalg, a German Protestant missionary sent by the Danes in 1706. He set up India's first printing press here and translated the New Testament into Tamil, laying the groundwork for modern Tamil prose literature.

By the 19th century, as colonial competition intensified, the Danes lost interest. In 1845, they sold their Indian holdings to the British. Tranquebar faded back into the quiet fishing village it had once been, but Fort Dansborg remained—a remnant of a European ambition far gentler and less invasive than others.

Today, the fort is beautifully preserved, its mustard-yellow facade standing against blue waves and whiter skies. A small museum within recounts the history of Danish India, and Tranquebar itself has become a heritage destination—its old churches, missionary schools, and tiled colonial houses offering a glimpse into an unexpected past.

Epilogue: Beyond 60

Even as we draw the curtain on this journey through stone, shadow, and sovereignty, the echoes do not end. India's forts—more than mere remnants of the past—are breathing archives, each holding a thousand untold stories. And for every one of the sixty we've chronicled in this volume, there are many others waiting just beyond the margins of selection. This is not an omission—it is an invitation. The journey, we hope, continues for you.

Consider, for instance, Hari Parbat Fort in Srinagar—a crown placed upon a hill already sacred for centuries. Long before Afghan governors built battlements there, the people of Kashmir revered it as Sharika Parbat, the home of their guardian goddess. When you stand atop its ramparts, looking out over Dal Lake and the old city, you're not just occupying a former garrison—you're standing at the confluence of power, faith, and geography. It is one of many such forts that straddle not only kingdoms, but cosmologies.

Travel farther south and you may encounter Bahu Fort in Jammu, another structure that blurs the boundary between fortification and temple. Believed to have been originally built over 3,000 years ago by Raja Bahulochan, and later restored by Dogra rulers, Bahu is less about grandeur and more about continuity. The Bawe Wali Mata Temple, housed within its walls, remains a site of devotion, where the sacred and the defensive continue to coexist.

We did not enter Chandragiri Fort in Andhra Pradesh, though it once held the destinies of empires. It was here that the Vijayanagara kings made their last stand before the capital shifted from Hampi. With its elegant Raja Mahal, now a museum, and its untouched surroundings, Chandragiri is a poignant whisper from a time that chose grace over vengeance in retreat.

Nor did we tread the forest paths to Ita Fort in Arunachal Pradesh—a lesser-known jewel of the Northeast. Built by the Ahom-related rulers of the region, its name literally means 'fort of bricks,' and its scale is immense. Yet it remains largely absent from national memory, tucked as it is within the hills and histories of a frontier land.

In Haryana, the Asigarh Fort (Hansi Fort) calls out through centuries. Once a pivotal outpost under the Tomars, later passed to the Mughals and Marathas, it is said to contain hidden vaults of ancient coins. Excavations have revealed rich layers of habitation, but time has not been as generous to its walls as it has to its legends.

We couldn't reach Kolaba Fort either—anchored off the coast of Alibag and accessible only at low tide. Once commanded by Shivaji Maharaj, the fort rises straight out of the Arabian Sea, flanked by bastions that still recall cannon smoke and monsoon storms. A maritime fort with temple and trident intact, Kolaba stands as a testament to the Maratha naval imagination.

Bahu, Hari Parbat, Chandragiri, Ita, Asigarh, Kolaba—they are just the beginning of the list that stretches beyond our final page. There is Fort Sewri in Mumbai, taken over by flamingoes and time. There are hilltop retreats like Rai Pithora Fort in Delhi and battle-scarred plains like Kalna Fort in Bengal. There is Batukeshwar Dham, where revolutionary Bhagat Singh once hid, and Lakhpat Fort, guarding the salt deserts of Kutch. There is Chunar, Chikhaldara, Basavakalyan, Umarkot, and so many more.

Some lie in ruins, eaten by vines. Some have been gently restored, turned into museums or boutique retreats. Some still house temples and traditions. Some host festivals. Some are vanishing silently, without even a signboard to mark their names.

But each of them deserves a visit. A pause. A question. A quiet walk along a crumbling rampart, wondering who once stood there—and why they built what they built. Because in India, forts were never just about war. They were about memory. About survival. About power and prayer, often side by side. They were palaces, prisons, temples, observatories, marketplaces, and sanctuaries.

We chose sixty. But we know—deeply and with humility—that the number was only a frame. The story cannot be contained.

So let this not be the end. Let this be the start of your own fort story. Open a map. Follow a ridge. Take the wrong turn. Ask the villagers. Let the ruins surprise you. Let silence speak.

For beyond the sixty forts you've read about here, lie six hundred more. And each one is waiting to be remembered.

Title: One Amazing Fort at a Time
Author: Ena Vismay

ISBN: 978-93-49042-35-3

Published by:
JGS Enterprises Pvt Ltd
Imprint: The Browser

Publisher's Address:
SCO 14-15, FF, Sector 8-C, Chandigarh 160 009
Website: thebrowser.org
Email: service@thebrowser.org

Printed in India

© Layout and Cover Design by beagles
99beagles.com

To the Aspiring Explorer Who Comes Next

Dear Wayfarer of Stones and Stories,

Somewhere, in the quiet hours between your routines and responsibilities, you must have felt it—that unplaceable pull, that ache for ruins, for ramparts, for wind whispering through a window carved five centuries ago. That feeling is real. And it is not new. You are walking a path that countless others have tread—kings, saints, rebels, traders, poets, all pulled by the same instinct: to climb, to stand at the edge of a fort wall, and to look out not just at land, but at time itself.

If you're reading this, perhaps you've already stood before the Red Fort and imagined the echoes of independence. Perhaps you've wandered through Mehrangarh's sandstone corridors or heard the silence at Daulatabad where prisoners once lay shackled. Or maybe you haven't yet begun. Maybe your feet are still on the verge of that first dusty trail.

Wherever you are on this journey, let this be your compass: India's forts are not just architecture—they are arguments, dreams, scars, and songs.

In their foundations lie the fury of defense and the longing for permanence. In their courtyards, kings have deliberated justice and plotted betrayals. Some walls were built to keep invaders out; others were built to trap daughters within. Some forts house temples older than time, while others hold bullet holes barely a century old. Some rose by rivers, others hid in forests, others still clung to hilltops as if to speak directly with the gods.

And yet, no matter how mighty they once were, every fort now shares one thing in common: they endure only if you care to remember them.

You may not find glossy signboards or curated gift shops. Sometimes you'll find goats. Or a school in session. Or nothing but wind. But if you wait, if you walk slowly, the fort will speak to you. In the way its stones heat up under the afternoon sun. In the echo of your own footsteps on the stairs. In the sudden realization that a queen once stood where you're standing now, staring at the same bend of the river.

So go. Take the narrow road. Ask for directions. Stay longer than you meant to. Visit not just the majestic giants—like Gwalior and Golconda—but the forgotten ones too: the forts that no longer boast, that do not charge entry, that survive by memory alone. Bring a notebook. Or don't. Just walk. Just look.

You are not merely a tourist. You are a keeper of continuity. A witness. A link between the past and the present. A traveler of the truest kind—not just across geography, but across time.

This book has given you sixty. But the land holds so many more. Find them. Climb them. Listen to them.

They've been waiting.

With dusty affection and a well-worn map,
A fellow explorer